GOD

AND

PSYCHOBABBLE

Know the truth!!

Blessings

Kathy

KATHY MARTIN

DESTINY IMAGE® PUBLISHERS, INC.

P.O. Box 310, Shippensburg, PA 17257-0310

"Promoting Inspired Lives."

This book and all other Destiny Image, Revival Press, MercyPlace, Fresh Bread, Destiny Image Fiction, and Treasure House books are available at Christian bookstores and distributors worldwide.

For a U.S. bookstore nearest you, call **1-800-722-6774.**

For more information on foreign distributors, call **717-532-3040.**

Reach us on the Internet: **www.destinyimage.com.**

ISBN 13 TP: 978-0-7684-4122-2

ISBN 13 Ebook: 978-0-7684-8839-5

For Worldwide Distribution, Printed in the U.S.A.

1 2 3 4 5 6 7 8 9 10 11 / 13 12

DEDICATION

*To Ron
How do I love thee?
I can't begin to count the ways.*

ACKNOWLEDGMENTS

For several years the Lord had laid on my heart and mind the title of a book, *God and Psychobabble*. I was so slow to realize that I was to write this book, and I am grateful that God was so patient in continuing to nudge me forward. Then my dear friend and author Jackie Kendall was the one who finally encouraged me to sit down at my computer, begin to write, and see what happens! Four months later to our surprise I had birthed the rough draft of *God and Psychobabble*. I am so grateful that she initially encouraged me and was there for me throughout this journey.

I am also so thankful to my husband Ron, who never wavered in his certainty and encouragement that I should write this book. He cooked, did laundry, picked up Chinese food when needed, and encouraged me lovingly when it was time to leave the computer and get some rest. He has always provided the balance I need. I could not have accomplished this work without his help. I appreciate my daughters for reading chapters and encouraging me to write when I proclaimed I was a psychotherapist, not an author. They gave me a confidence that I simply did not have on my own.

I appreciate my dear clients who over the years taught me through their pain and tears far more than I could ever teach them. And oh how I appreciate God's most marvelous instruction manual, His Word. It has been the key to my private practice, as the principles in that book WORK!

And finally, I must thank a myriad of wonderful pastors, Bible teachers and professionals who trained me in Biblical and psychological principles. They include Dr. Warren Wiersbe, Dr. Charles Stanley, Frank Minirth, M.D., Paul Meier, M.D., Dr. John MacArthur, Dr. James Dobson, Dr. Patrick Mulhall, Dr. Earl Comfort, Bible teacher Jackie Kendall and Bible Study Fellowship. Finally I appreciate my publisher Destiny Image for taking a chance on a new author, and Terri Meckes for working with me with gentle patience.

ENDORSEMENTS

Kathy Martin has been a lifesaver for my wife personally and for our marriage. Her use of God's Word through counseling is truly astounding.

Heath Evans
NFL, New Orleans Saints, Linebacker
President of Heath Evans Foundation for
Victims of Childhood Sexual Abuse

This book is an excellent resource for therapists as well as clients! Kathy Martin has taken popular psychological concepts and evaluated their merit based on Scripture. She clearly presents life-changing biblical principles and their applications to common problems. This wonderful book will equip therapists to practice from a biblical perspective and will help clients to navigate their difficulties from a scriptural foundation.

Julie Hamilton, PhD, LMFT
Licensed Marriage and Family Therapist

If truth is what "sets you free," then logically what holds you captive is deception. Spiritually and emotionally, we are inmates to subtle lies and are held hostage by the invisible chains of falsehood—not so much the lies we tell, but the ones we believe. We are jailed by our silent acceptance of the flawed reasonings whispered to us by our past, others, the world, and the great liar.

With great insight and care, Martin gently helps us expose the hidden deceptions that bind us to discouragement, anxiety, resentment, and other maladies. Then she expertly guides us in replacing the subtle and false with the clear and true.

Martin has done us a great service with this book. Our hearts, our lives, and our relationships will be the blessed and grateful beneficiaries.

Ramon Presson, MS
Therapist and Author of
When Will My Life Not Suck? Authentic Hope for the Disillusioned

Kathy Martin's description of major issues dealt with in counseling is refreshing! She continually goes back to biblical truth as the key to understanding people. A must-read for those who take a biblical worldview when dealing with people in pain.

Elizabeth Skjoldal, PhD
Director MACP Trinity International University Florida Regional Center and Licensed Psychologist

TABLE OF
CONTENTS

FOREWORD

It is with great joy that I write this foreword for a book that flows from the heart of the wisest counselor I have ever known. I have been in ministry for three decades, and I have been a witness to the emotional bondage that comes when a person frames his or her life with debilitating psychobabble rather than the liberating truth of God. I have witnessed so many people living a generic version of their real life because of the emotional crippling they experience through believing half-truths that are not truth at all.

God and Psychobabble exposes the lies that keep so many people emotionally crippled. Kathy Martin has spent decades sharing truths with men and women who have suffered from receiving superficial treatment for their soul's struggle. Psychobabble does not liberate people from their common struggles: stress, anxiety, depression, addiction, suffering, loneliness, divorce, etc. Such "pop psychology" is a Band-Aid on a mortal wound.

What sets this book apart from others is the unique insight that Kathy Martin has in confronting the psychobabble that is a verbal gibberish, and replacing this debilitating babble with life-changing truths that *work*! Each chapter contains a clever confrontation of the lies that fuel psychobabble, and the results are energizing and therapeutic.

God and Psychobabble contains truths expressed so candidly that one will begin to experience freedom with the turn of each page. Whether contending with anger, disappointment, stress, or depression, clarity is inevitable. The reader will have so many "ah-ha" moments that there will be drool on his or her shirt.

Kathy Martin's advice and counsel have always been so practical that anyone with an open mind and heart can grasp and apply the insights that flow through her brilliant soul. The concepts that she shares with passion are transferable. Many of her clients have encouraged others with the insight they gain from spending time with her. These transferable concepts are so unique and profound that they are easy to remember. The insights in this book will help the reader put an end to self-sabotaging choices and skewed self-talk.

For decades Kathy Martin has been a counselor for thousands, and it can be said of her, she gives counsel *"like that of one who inquires of God"* (2 Sam. 16:23). I have sent so many people to her for counseling that I considered having her office number tattooed on my wrist! This book is a must for anyone involved in soul care—whether it is your soul that needs liberation or the souls of others. I am so excited that you are going to benefit from all the wisdom that God has trusted Kathy with—and you don't have to get on a plane and fly to her office in South Florida.

Jackie Kendall,
Best-Selling Author of *Lady in Waiting*

INTRODUCTION

People love *psychobabble!* Look at our talk shows and bookstore shelves. Media favorites include Dr. Phil, Dr. Laura, and *The Oprah Winfrey Show,* just to name a few. People are turning new shows on from *In Treatment* to *Celebrity Rehab* to *The Sober House.* People can't get enough of the self-help books geared to probe the psyche, resolve your problems, and straighten out your life. And I must admit that I too am looking to help each person to have more of the "life and life abundant" I believe God wants for us. I thoroughly believe in efforts to make the mind well. After all, the mind is the command center for the entire body. And how can we have any real quality of life when the mind is in a perpetual state of sadness, fear, or torment?

Furthermore, clinical studies and observations have convinced researchers that many physical illnesses are actually *psychogenic,* which simply means that worry, family, and work-related stress or unconscious needs can greatly contribute to a person's physical illnesses, which contributes to the onset of future diseases of all kinds. This link has become so profound that a new area of study has surfaced called *psychoneuroimmunology,* which attempts to determine how stress affects the immune system, which opens the door to viral or bacterial infection. While Socrates was certainly not privy to the medical technology of today, even he had the insight to state, "Just as you ought not attempt to cure eyes without head or head without body, so you should not treat the body without the soul."[1]

But what is psychobabble, what is the role of psychobabble, and is it helpful? Mr. Webster defines it as "employing language and concepts of psychology in a superficial way."[2] And since *superficial* means "concerned with and understanding only the easy, apparent and obvious; not profound; shallow,"[3] our world is currently groaning and suffering from the logical consequences of our obsession with psychobabble. Why? Because *shallow* doesn't cut it. It doesn't answer the longings of the human heart. It only reflects the condition of the human heart. And if psychobabble is today's answer to the world's walking wounded, does anyone hear the subtle foolishness with the term "self help"?

Psychobabble deals with the momentary relief, the quick fix, and the feel-good remedy. As a counselor of many years, I've found that people often want only to come to my office to vent their anger or frustrations with a person or a situation. They're not always interested in rolling up their sleeves, going deeper, resolving the issue, and finding the *truth* in each matter. They're only interested in rehearsing their situation, polishing it up, and accepting it as truth—their truth.

Psychobabble can be a marvelous aid in this journey. It has the potential to skirt depth, elevate pride, and keep us going around in circles like a hamster on a wheel, going nowhere, accomplishing only exhaustion, emptiness, and a continual search for relief from our pain. It focuses on all the popular catch phrases and issues like codependence, denial, dysfunction, self-actualization, empowerment, etc., rather than dealing with the deeper issue of the heart in all of these matters. Please let it be noted that I use those phrases in my office each day because they absolutely are a manifestation of where we are and therefore need to be addressed. The key here is where's the *truth?*

I have come to the conclusion that *all* of the problems that enter my office occur due to some kind of *lie* that has infiltrated the brain. I now sit and wait, listening to an individual's pain, and like a prospector waiting for that little nugget of gold, I excitedly anticipate the moment when the lies begin to surface. I regularly use an analogy in my office that most of us can probably relate to. I am unfortunately a true lover of chocolate. If I went to my next doctor visit and he told me that chocolate chip cookies really didn't have many calories or cholesterol, that it was just a hoax perpetrated by the Anti-Chocolate League, and if I believed the lie, I would make a race to the nearest bakery and begin to load up! But what would the consequence be? I would put on 20 pounds, and my cholesterol would shoot to the moon all within the span of a month! Continued belief in the lie would result in none of my clothes fitting and an insistence by my doctor that I should be on anti-cholesterol medication.

This is exactly what occurs in my office every day. People entertain a lie, enjoy what the lie tells them about themselves or life, embrace the lie as truth, manifest actions and choices based on the lie, and are then crushed when their belief results in a train wreck! What does the train wreck look like? Families not speaking to one another, loneliness, divorces in record numbers, substance abuse, out–of-control children, charge cards that look more like mortgages, depression and anxiety accompanied by depression and anxiety medications sold in record quantities, etc.

Years ago, I heard Ann Graham Lotz state that if Prozac were around during the time of King David, we would have missed out on all his profound words of struggle as well as joy. Our medications often numb us, dulling our senses to the exciting journey of life with all its mountains and valleys. But they are incredibly popular in today's world. Is this because we no longer want to feel or because we just want the easy way out?

Oh, if only the easy way worked I would personally advocate it to each one of my clients over these many years. But I'm far too practical a gal. Unfortunately, the easy way often does nothing more than mask the truth, making it possible for us to remain in the shallowness of our day-to-day world. This is not to say that there isn't a time for medications, but too often they are mistaken as the *remedy* rather than a *tool* to help us reach the greater goal of knowing the truth that will truly set us free (see John 8:32).

I believe the first time we probably see an example of *psychobabble* is in Genesis 11. The early Babylonians all had the same language at this time in history. These people were given clear directions by God, but decided to reject God's plans for their own "better" choices. Warren Wiersbe states, "Man seeks unity and notoriety, and he tries to accomplish these things by his own wisdom and strength."[4] Am I hearing the beginning of a *lie* that might lead to disaster? Is it possible that man could actually think that his plans might be better than the plans of the one who created the universe?

So the people of Babylon decided to build a tower to the heavens "so that we may make a name for ourselves and not be scattered over the face of the whole earth."[5] This was contrary to God's instructions, to God's plan for humankind. So God came to the earth and confused the language so that they were unable to communicate with one another. This resulted is humanity being scattered all over the earth, which was God's original plan.

> *Come, let Us go down and confuse their language so they will not understand each other* (Genesis 11:7).

> *That is why it was called Babel—because there the Lord confused the language of the whole world. From there*

the Lord scattered them over the face of the whole earth (Genesis 11:9).

So the Tower of Babel ended. The word *Babel* means "confusion."[6] When people choose their *own* way, the result will be one of confusion, because the foundation of their belief that our way is better than God's way is a *lie* rather than *truth*. The Babylonians wanted life *their* way, and the result was confusion. They could no longer communicate with one another, which resulted in them becoming distanced from one another, first physically and eventually relationally.

The choice of *psychobabble* as *humanity's* way to deal with life and all of its difficulties and complications will inevitably result in the same confusion that the Babylonians faced: unable to communicate deeply, resolving nothing, but communicating only in a superficial and shallow manner. The result will be a distancing from one another, first relationally and then physically. Once again Warren Wiersbe's words of wisdom state, "Wherever there is confusion, the spirit of Babylon—the world and the flesh—is at work."[7] The search for a *truth* of *our* own "dead ends" into a lie, and a life built on a lie in the brain "dead ends" into a life filled with confusion, depression, anxiety, etc. This is the world of *psychobabble*.

I believe people really desire an abundant life, but the question is, are they willing to work through releasing *their truth* in favor of *God's truth* to achieve it?

Chapter 1

THE TRUTH ABOUT
CODEPENDENCE

How could we possibly write a psychobabble book without a chapter on codependence! Why? Because while I see codependence in my office every day, I can't help but see it as a perfect complement to psychobabble. Once again we ask, *why?* Because if you recall from our introduction, psychobabble was defined as "employing language and concepts of psychology in a superficial way." This is exactly the way the world deals with codependence. While many nonreligious people see their codependence as a problem that practically defines their lives, lives that are filled with meetings and self-analysis, many religious people are treating codependence as foolishness. Where is the *truth*? Where is the lie?

WHAT IS CODEPENDENCE?

Let's begin by understanding what codependence is. Melody Beattie's book *Codependent No More* has been very helpful in sorting out many of the specifics of this word that cannot be found in Mr. Webster's "big book." The term *codependency* was coined in the late 1970s and originally referred to alcohol-related dependence. Melody Beattie's definition is far more comprehensive. She states, "A codependent person is one who has let another person's behavior affect him or her, and who is obsessed with controlling that person's behavior."[1]

I agree with this definition of a problem that plagues so many people and robs them of a contented, abundant life while thrusting them into a far more stressful and complicated one. We see in this definition a "bi-directional" movement, an ebb and flow pattern. The person who has allowed another's behavior to affect them now wants to become the person who will do the controlling. The controlled now wants to become the controller, and back and forth they move. This continual back-and-forth relational movement is an exhausting way to live.

Where I differ with this traditional understanding of codependence compared to the *truth* of codependence is with the *why* and prevalence of codependence.

To begin with, *codependence*—letting another person's behavior affect us and grasping to control that person's behavior—is at the very core of *every* man and woman's nature and heart. Why do I say this? For two very clear reasons, both of which we will explore.

CREATED TO BE IN RELATIONSHIP

The first reason is that we were created by a Creator to be in relationship with a living God. Interconnected relationship is the heart's cry for every person on earth. Relationship is defined as "the quality or state of being related; connection."[2] God created us to connect first with Him and then with others. However, God wouldn't create us to be in a relationship with Him and not put longings in our heart to seek the fulfillment of that relationship or connectedness. This is because *God never asks something of us without equipping us with tools or abilities to achieve what He desires.* Hence, we were created for "relational dependence," not for "relational independence."

Logic would therefore dictate that whether it be in marriage, blood, friendship, etc., if we were created to be relationally connected, how could our deeper heart longings for that connectedness that we were created to seek not give that other person some degree of power to affect our behavior in some profound way? We are connected—*created in dependence rather than independence!* Therefore, interdependence and allowing another to have some effect on our behavior is perfectly logical. Our very creation cries out to this understanding of dependency and connectedness.

> *The Lord God formed the man from the dust of the ground and breathed into his nostrils the breath of life, and the man became a living being* (Genesis 2:7).

> *For You created my inmost being; You knit me together in my mother's womb. I praise You because I am fearfully and wonderfully made; Your works are wonderful, I know that full well. My frame was not hidden from You when I was made in the secret place, when I was woven together in the depths of the earth. Your eyes saw my unformed body...* (Psalm 139:13-16).

> *O Lord, You have searched me and You know me. You know when I sit and when I rise; You perceive my thoughts from afar. You discern my going out and my lying down; You are familiar with all my ways. Before a word is on my tongue You know it completely, O Lord. You hem me in—behind and before; You have laid your hand upon me. Such knowledge is too wonderful for me, too lofty for me to attain. Where can I go from Your Spirit? Where can I flee from Your presence?* (Psalm 139:1-7).

Wow, do those last verses sound like a connected relationship?

We are a species created to be in relationship with God Himself first, born dependent on God, and second to be in relationship with one another. This is made clear when we view Adam in the Garden. At the beginning of time, God made Adam first. God and Adam communicated with one another regularly in the Garden of Eden. But in Genesis 2:18 God said, *"It is not good for the man to be alone. I will make a helper suitable for him."* This tells us that Adam *did not do well alone.* While God is certainly sufficient for our needs, there must have been something God saw that Adam needed. Perhaps it was simply the need for physical touch, since God was spirit.

Whatever it was, it still exists today because we too have a need for physical interaction with others as well as relationship connectedness. Many sweet volunteers enter nursing homes simply to hold the hands of our elderly who no longer receive that desperately needed physical touch from loved ones who might be deceased or who live in other states. Pet therapy has also become very popular in nursing homes. Dogs often provide an unconditional love for whoever will scratch their bellies, making a lonely person feel loved and connected.

PRIDE REALISTICALLY WANTS TO CONTROL

The second reason that the definition for codependence is at the very core of the heart of every man and woman has to do with the second part of Ms. Beattie's definition of codependence. It states that the person who has been affected by another is now obsessed with controlling the controller. This is absolutely realistic. There's that word again—realistic—that separates *truth* from *lie*. It is realistic and natural for a person to be obsessed with controlling others. How do we know this? Because we were all born into sin with a nature that is filled with *pride*. And *pride* wants its own way! Pride wants to control!

I will continually be going back to the Garden of Eden for our examples, as it is there we see our very first man and woman. After a bit of historical study, it is clear that their examples are alive and well today. As King Solomon stated in Ecclesiastes 1:9:

> *What has been will be again, what has been done will be done again; there is nothing new under the sun.*

Adam and Eve were created individually by a perfect God. God gave them perfection in the Garden of Eden. Genesis 3:8 even states that God Himself actually walked with them in the Garden. They enjoyed perfect weather and perfect food, every animal just sat at their feet for their enjoyment, and even work in the garden was not frustrating because originally there were no weeds. According to Genesis 3:18, it was only after man sinned that weeds began to pop up. Originally, they were in charge of the entire garden. God gave them one simple *no!*

> *And the Lord God commanded the man, "You are free to eat from any tree in the garden; but you must not eat from the tree of the knowledge of good and evil, for when you eat of it you will surely die"* (Genesis 2:16-17).

Now both Adam and Eve knew full well that eating from this one tree was strictly taboo. But what was it this couple just had to obsess over? Of course, it was the only thing they did not have complete control over! Why? Because their hearts were filled with *pride,* and they weren't content until they did it their way! Attempting to control others is in my estimation *realistic* because man is born into sin and pride. It is *unrealistic,* and once again I'm hearing the whisper of that little lie to think that man in his basic nature is not going to attempt to control others.

This controlling behavior is also made clear in Eve's attempt to control Adam's behavior in Genesis 3:6:

When the woman saw that the fruit of the tree was good for food and pleasing to the eye, and also desirable for gaining [knowledge], *she took some and ate it. She also gave some to her husband, who was with her, and he ate it.*

Did Adam allow her behavior to affect him? Absolutely!

Yet another way we see this *truth* manifested is to observe the behavior of any toddler on the planet! If Toddler Tommy wants Sister Susie's toy, he will first try the "grab and run." If he gets stopped by some cruel authority, Mom perhaps, he will probably try the "cry and pity me" approach next. If that doesn't work, he will probably circle his unsuspecting prey, Sister Susie, and the moment she puts down the toy, he'll declare victory because he knows Mom will let him have it if he acquired the toy fair and square: "She put it down, Mom!" Then, after playing with it for about 60 seconds, he'll move on to the next "forbidden fruit"! Toddler Tommy observed his sister playing with her toy, and in pride decided he wanted to take control of her toy for himself. Any mother sees this played out daily.

CODEPENDENCE: DISORDER AND THE HEART OF MAN

Now this by itself should not imply that we're all living a dysfunctional, codependent lifestyle. This is where our *psychobabble* and *truth* are separated. *Psychobabble* again is defined as "employing language and concepts of psychology in a superficial way." Superficially defining codependence, or seeing it through the eyes of psychobabble, would be to define what is the most obvious, not profound, shallow, and superficial observations concerning humankind. Psychobabble sees codependence as a *disorder* rather than the deeper issue that defines the very nature and creation of humankind. Psychobabble sees codependence as a disorder rather than a *demonstration* of humanity's need for God as well as a demonstration of humanity's sinful and prideful nature.

Man *is* a codependent creature, as Melody Beattie describes codependence as both "letting another person's behavior affect him or her, and who is obsessed with controlling that person's behavior." The *world* and psychobabble want to foolishly view man as an inherently independent creature rather than the weak and fragile humans that we truly are. The *world* and *psychobabble* want to view our "attachment" and "controlling" issues as some kind of disorder rather than the heart of humankind.

By making codependence a disorder rather than a biblical *captain-obvious* moment, it becomes one more quiet way of separating man and woman from God. By making our attachment and codependence issues a disorder, humanity can justify their prideful desire to stand alone without any need for a power above themselves. The desire to free ourselves from any kind of codependence is simply another subtle and psychobabble therapeutic way to detach ourselves from God's greater plan of connectedness as found in principles such as the "helpmate principle" found in Genesis 2:18, the "sacrificial love principle" found in First John 3:16, and the "considering others more important than ourselves principle" from Philippians 2:3, just to name a few. The prideful heart of humanity wants this to be a disorder because *pride* desires to stand alone. *Pride* wants to be at the top of the food chain, *not* being affected by others.

I am a fan of AA, or Alcoholics Anonymous, and Alanon, which is an offshoot of AA designed to aid family members of alcoholics. I have seen so many people tremendously helped by these programs. I have worked with many family members of alcoholics who have faithfully attended Alanon. My only issue with this program, however, is the *degree* of detachment of the individual or family to the alcoholic. The program so focuses on the "problem" of being codependent with the alcoholic that they err on the side of too strong a "detachment."

For example, how does the wife of an alcoholic completely detach from her ill husband and remain the biblical helpmate she was designed to be? How does the adult son of an alcoholic mother completely detach from his mom and still show her the respect called for in the fifth commandment? How does one allow the continued sin of an alcoholic spouse to profoundly affect the lives of the children and not *confront* and possibly *deal* with that sin according to the principle of Matthew 18:15?

THE REAL QUESTION IS, WHO ARE WE CODEPENDENT WITH?

I believe the answer is not so much based on whether we are codependent or not codependent, but rather **who are we codependent with?** It *is* our natural bent to be codependent—to be affected by others and then to desire to control their behavior. Therefore, our wellness is far more determined by *who* are we codependent with rather than *if* we are codependent.

Look at the logic this presents. When I am codependent to an alcoholic or drug user, wow, will my life be one volatile and dysfunctional mess. The life of a person on drugs or alcohol is perpetually filled with chaos, heartbreak, fights, rages, money conflicts, lies, etc. We might let their alcohol use put us in a depression or an angry rage. We might take our frustration out on our children. Some have quietly exited the marriage by having an affair as an unhealthy way of "detaching" from the alcoholic. We have allowed them to affect our behavior, all right, just as Melody Beattie describes in her definition, "a codependent person is one who has let another person's behavior affect him or her."

Afterward, we're filled with guilt and end up hating ourselves, so we yell ultimatums to the alcoholic that he or she *must* stop the drinking right *now or else!* That is so unrealistic. We treat the alcoholic with anger or disdain, trying to break him or her down so he or she will finally get help and change his or her behaviors! We are now living the second half of Melody Beattie's codependent definition as we are obsessed with trying to control the other person's behavior. The truth is that no one is able to control another's behavior. While we know that God alone is all powerful to control what He wants to control, He has chosen to give each of us a *free will*.

ALLEY AND JANICE

Alley had rather low self-esteem in high school and was hoping things would be different in college. But her insecurity followed her to college, where she felt fearful and insecure. Alley's roommate, Janice, was a rather controlling young woman, and it didn't take long for Alley to develop a codependent relationship with her roommate.

First semester freshman year finds Alley and Janice almost inseparable, but by their second semester, Alley finds a new friend and would actually like to pursue a friendship with this young woman. Janice becomes jealous and irritated if Alley even hints at a friendship with this new girl from class. Alley and her new friend want to go out to lunch together, but Alley is fearful to mention the lunch date to Janice, so Alley lies about her whereabouts. Afterward, Alley hates herself for being so controlled by Janice that she would actually lie about something she has every right to do—go out to lunch!

Alley, in her frustration, begins to act in a cold manner with Janice, almost trying to pick a fight and possibly turn the tables on her. Alley is angry at Janice for being so controlling, and she's angry at herself for allowing Janice to affect so much of her own behavior. She tries to alter or control Janice by pouting and appearing cold, and on and on the cycle goes. Here we see a classic example of codependence where a person (Alley) has let another person (Janice) affect her behavior and that person (Alley) is now obsessed with controlling that other person's (Janice's) behavior.

ANN AND JONATHAN

What about Ann and her husband Jonathan? They are a sweet Christian couple who are very much in love and who appear to have a strong marriage. But when he comes home in a bad mood because he's had to lay off a worker, he becomes withdrawn and quiet. Ann begins to take his withdrawal personally, feeling that he's shutting her out of his life. She becomes sullen, hoping that her reaction to his withdrawal will cause him to give her attention. When that's unsuccessful, she begins to make sarcastic comments about him "just leaving her out whenever he wants," now trying to force him to respond to her in a more communicative manner. She's allowed him to affect her behavior, and she now tries to control his behavior.

In both circumstances we see codependence, but clearly the first example is easily labeled codependent and dysfunctional. The college roommate example appears rather unhealthy, but it doesn't scream "codependent" at us. In our second example, we could almost call Ann and Jonathan normal newlyweds, but in each case we are seeing the principles of codependency unfold. Humanity's simple-birthed nature is codependent with others. The codependent has let another person's behavior affect him or her, and then he or she is obsessed with controlling that person's behavior.

VARIOUS LEVELS OF CODEPENDENCE

Now, are there various levels of codependence? Absolutely! And at what point would we consider the codependence to be truly problematic? I do believe that the more dysfunction people have endured in their family of origin, the less secure they will be in their own skin, which causes them to allow others to affect their behavior far more than the person from a secure family of origin, which creates less of an allowance to be controlled by others. Therefore, we can conclude that the level of dysfunction in one's life concerning any given circumstance can definitely parallel with how problematic the codependence could be. But as we stated earlier, wouldn't that then be directly connected to *who* we are codependent with? Whoever the codependent connects to would have to inadvertently gauge the severity of the problematic and dysfunctional level of the codependence. Let's investigate.

We've already established that it is man's natural bent to be relationally connected and therefore "affected to some degree by others," and we've established man's natural bent to control others due to the sin of pride. We've also seen from our two examples that the degree of dysfunction in our lives is closely aligned to *who* we are codependent with rather than *if* we are codependent, because there is no *if* we are codependent; we simply *are*.

HORIZONTAL CODEPENDENCE

Now let's take a closer look at this aspect of *who* we are codependent with. We begin by realizing that when we become codependent with any other person on earth, we are choosing a *horizontal* codependence or a connectedness with a person other than ourselves. This simply means we are choosing a connectedness with a person who is just as drenched in sin as we are. The logical conclusion to such a relationship is that we now not only have to deal with our own sin nature, but we end up being affected by the other person's sin nature as well. For example, if the other person is jealous, we will be affected by his or her jealousy. If he or she has an anger problem, we will be affected by his or her anger. If he or she has a spirit of fear, we will be affected by his or her fearfulness.

VERTICAL CODEPENDENCE

But do you realize what happens if we choose to be *vertically* codependent? Vertically codependent simply means *choosing* to be codependent with the Lord Himself, the King of kings and Lord of lords.

We will be choosing a vertical codependence with a God who is sinless, perfect, and immutable—which simply means He never changes! This is profound and logical at the same time. Imagine being codependent with the Lord and allowing His behavior to affect us and then being obsessed with controlling Him. What on earth would **codependence with the King** look like?

CODEPENDENCE WITH THE KING

For just one moment, imagine, intentionally choosing to have the Lord affect our behavior. Codependence with God! Essentially, that means we would attempt to get all of our marching orders from God or God's Word. Remember, John 1:1 states, *"In the beginning was the Word, and the Word was with God, and the Word **was** God."* That means if we get our marching orders from the Bible, they are God's instructions. Since God never sins, we are getting our marching orders from one who never sins and who would never steer us toward a wrong, cruel, sarcastic, hurtful, or evil behavior. Since every person on this earth sins—from the raging alcoholic to the loving parent—humans will inevitably aim us in the direction of sin; they can't help it because we all have a sin nature! Paul himself declared this:

> *I know that nothing good lives in me, that is, in my sinful nature. For I have the desire to do what is good, but I cannot carry it out. For what I do is not the good I want to do; no, the evil I do not want to do—this I keep on doing* (Romans 7:18-19).

When we are codependent with any other person in any "horizontal" relationship, we are actually being affected by or reactive to a sinner, which logically causes us to be more likely to sin. If we are codependent with the Lord Himself, we will be affected by or reactive to one who is sinless, which would logically cause us to sin less.

We also know that one of God's attributes is that He is immutable, which means He never changes. Can you imagine how peaceful and sane life would be when we attach and are affected by one who never has mood swings, jealousy issues, and irritation due to lack of sleep or failure to get that job promotion? One who never has hormonal swings or mid-life crises? Can you imagine attaching to one who doesn't change His mind or opinion, leaving us wondering or unsure what our feedback will be? Can you imagine being relationally connected to one who is never volatile, frantic, or emotionally immature and who is as steady in His convictions as a rock and who will never leave or forsake us? He is one we can always count on to affect our behavior in a way that will help us to exhibit *"love, joy, peace, patience, kindness, goodness, faithfulness, gentleness and self-control"* (Gal. 5:22-23)!

RUN INTO HIS ARMS

The *truth* is that we should *run* with wild abandon to the only one who is totally safe to be codependent with: the Lord Himself. When it comes to the first part of Melody Beattie's definition of *codependence*—"A codependent person is one who has let another person's behavior affect him or her"—who else but the Lord fits the bill with absolute perfection? Isn't it brilliantly logical that a perfect God who wanted us to have an abundant life would create in us the need to be dependent, and then supply Himself to us, to give us His very best shot at that well life?

Now let's tackle that second portion of our definition: "A codependent is one who has let another person's behavior affect him or her, *and who is obsessed with controlling that person's behavior."* What this means is that the very person whose behavior has been affected by another now becomes obsessed with controlling that person's behavior.

I believe we've already established the fact that humanity is *controlling*! If we're codependent with the Lord, we would conclude that we would be trying to control His behavior. **Well, *isn't that what the*** *majority of our prayers consist of?* We cry out to God for help with our broken dreams! We ask Him to heal our sick bodies! We ask Him to protect us when we take that airplane trip! We ask Him to give us healthy pregnancies and then healthy babies! We pray for God's perfect choice of a spouse to enter our lives! We ask Him to help get us that perfect job we want so badly and then ask Him to help us get the promotion or account we so desperately want! We ask Him to heal our broken marriage before it results in divorce!

Had our student Alley been *vertically codependent* with the Lord, she would not have been affected by Janice, would not have been fearful to disclose her new friendship, would have felt sad for Janice that she was struggling with jealousy or insecurity issues, would have gone to the Lord in prayer about the matter, might have possibly invited Janice to go to lunch with herself and her new friend, would have been open to talking about the issue with Janice rather than spiraling into angry places, etc.

Had our newlywed Ann been *vertically codependent* with the Lord, she would have tried to be a help to her husband while he struggled with the pain of having to let an employee go, would have communicated she was there should he need to talk about it, would have tried to give him the space he seemed to need without taking it personally, would have gone to the Lord and prayed for her husband, etc.

Vertical codependence with the Lord would give both Ann and Alley a more peaceful life, more healthy and realistic conclusions to their problems, as well as a closer walk with the Lord, which always results in a more joyful life.

I had the sweetest Christian lady in my office recently. Her greatest pleasures had been a combination of golf and tennis. However, she's been having serious problems with her adult son, who she believes is getting involved in a drug lifestyle. While he is an executive with a high-paying job, she knows what the future holds if he continues in his current direction, and her confrontation of the situation is causing a brokenhearted end to their relationship. She has been in a constant state of worry, has had trouble sleeping and functioning, etc. Her son is always a thought away. As we discussed the problem, I inquired how it has changed her life regarding her day-to-day activities. She was quick to respond that she's never spent as much time in prayer as she has these last several weeks. She's been desperately begging the Lord to help her son, to convict her son, to change his heart, etc.

DESPERATE PEOPLE
BIRTH PRAYER WARRIORS

While we tend to see control as a negative codependent issue, the *truth* is that it is our crying out to the Lord, our trying to convince Him to do things our way, and our days of begging and pleading that actually draw us into a deeper relationship with Him. Desperate people *birth prayer warriors*! And prayer warriors are some of the wisest and most joyful people I know because they're in a constant state of communication with the Lord.

With tears in her eyes, I asked this Christian lady if she thought her walk with God had changed because of her desperation. She was quick to share how wonderful it had been to feel God's presence so clearly in her life: "How my priorities have changed. What used to be my world is now of such little importance. I'm so constantly close to the Lord. I can't imagine living any other way."

So look at how that second part of Ms. Beattie's definition is so marvelous and relevant! She points out that the codependent (us) is the one who's let another person's behavior affect him or her (the other person would be God) and who becomes obsessed with controlling that person's behavior. (We become obsessed with controlling God's behavior when we regularly cry out to Him to change the direction of our life in alignment with our desires.)

This awesome cycle of *vertical codependence* not only accomplishes God's desire to establish a "relationship of dependence" with Him, but at the same time, our obsession to "control" God's decisions in our lives draws us desperately near to Him and gives us a more-fulfilling life than we could ever imagine. I have personally never desired or enjoyed the often-difficult road to *vertical codependence*. But I would never change one step of a walk that has provided more *freedom, joy,* and *dependence* on Him than I could ever imagine.

Codependence, man's way, or the way of *psychobabble* becomes just one more *horizontal mumbo mess* filled with confusion over boundaries, self–determination, and denial, *blah, blah, blah!* Codependence with the King! Bring it on! Give me more!

QUESTIONS

1) Most people are familiar with the term codependent, but not many people actually understand the term. What did you think the term meant prior to reading this chapter? What do you understand it to mean now?

2) Do you feel you or a family member was in some way involved in a codependent relationship with another person? Would you share that relationship with the group?

3) If so, would you describe some of the specific frustrations that would occur in such a relationship when being both "affected by the other person and then becoming obsessed with trying to control them?"

4) How might a codependent relationship with God actually help a current difficult human relationship?

5) How does having a codependent relationship with God help a person deal with another person's issues, such as anger issues, jealousy issues, alcohol issues, controlling issues, etc.

Chapter 2

THE TRUTH ABOUT
DEPRESSION: PART 1

Depression is one of the most common presenting problems for health professionals today. People are being prescribed medications for depression in record numbers, and prescriptions are being written not only by psychiatrists but by many gynecologists, internists, family physicians, urgent care clinics, etc.

It is estimated that depressive disorders affect approximately 9.5 percent of the U.S. adult population age 18 and older in a given year, while the rate of increase of depression among children is an astounding 23 percent. It is estimated that 30 percent of women are depressed and 15 percent of the population of most developed nations suffer severe depression. Forty-one percent of depressed women are too embarrassed to seek help, perhaps because 54 percent of people feel depression is a personal weakness. Eighty percent of depressed people are not seeking help, and sadly, 15 percent of depressed people will commit suicide. Depression results in more absenteeism than almost any other physical disorder and costs employers more than $51 billion a year in absenteeism and lost productivity, not including high medical and pharmaceutical bills. It is estimated that by the year 2020, depression will be the second largest killer after heart disease—and studies show that depression is a contributory factor to fatal coronary disease.[1]

Depressed patients are described as:

> Typically having a negative view of themselves, their environment, and the future. They view themselves as worthless, inadequate, unlovable, and deficient. Depressed patients view the environment as overwhelming, as presenting insuperable obstacles that cannot be overcome, and as continually resulting in failure or loss. Moreover, they view the future as hopeless; they believe their efforts will be insufficient to change the unsatisfying course of their life.[2]

Now I'm hoping that as you're reading this description, you're not identifying with too many of these negative circumstances. The truth is that hopeless, helpless, sadness feelings have been experienced by most everyone at one time or another in life. We all experience difficulties that slowly or suddenly plunge us into chaos, heartbreak, and shattered dreams. The medical diagnosis we dread, the financial reversal that leaves us panic-stricken, the untimely death of a loved one, the injustice done to an innocent child, and the broken relationship that was supposed to last a lifetime are just a few of the circumstances that can turn our world upside down. Jesus Himself told us in John 16:33, *"In this world you will have trouble."* His warning was accurate.

In the classic book *Happiness is a Choice* by doctors Frank B. Minirth and Paul D. Meier, they state:

> We have already seen that some adults are more prone to depression than others because of unhealthy family patterns, especially in the first six years of life. One of the main factors is being taught in childhood to repress

anger rather than learning to express anger tactfully and constructively. A less important factor is heredity.[3]

I couldn't agree with their assessment more. The issue here becomes the degree and length of depression that each one of us undergoes when confronted with life's difficulties. While some people will go several rounds with depressed thoughts but then circle back to well thinking, others can go a lifetime struggling with sadness and disappointment more days than not. What is it that causes one person to bounce back, or at least drag themselves back to well thinking, while another will remain trapped indefinitely?

UNREALISTIC EXPECTATIONS

In my years of practice, I have found that almost all depression, short term or long term, has a common denominator—*unrealistic expectations!* The numerators vary: relationship breakup, an adulterous spouse, financial loss, death of a loved one, unruly children, problems with parents or in-laws, etc. But I can always count on that denominator being the same—unrealistic expectations! And when we really look more closely at *unrealistic expectations,* what are we seeing? A *lie* of course! *Unreal* is defined as "not real, actual or genuine, imaginary, fanciful, false."[4]

The person who remains in the depression has bought into the *lie,* the negative view about themselves, life, God, their family, their friends, what they deserve in life, what they don't deserve in life, etc. Not only have they bought the *lie,* but they have also let the lie move into their guest room and then hang out with it during their morning coffee. They let the lie spin around in their brain during the course of the day. They give the lie legs during the afternoon and walk around with it, and then they take it to bed with them at night laying awake pondering and rehearsing it. Hours after a person has gone to sleep, the lie continues in the brain. Eventually, the lie has become so much a part of one's every thought every hour of every day that it becomes a person's *new normal*; the *lie* or *unrealistic expectation* becomes a person's *own truth!* Then when life doesn't turn out as a person expected it should have turned out based on his or her *own expectations,* which are actually *unrealistic,* the person becomes *disappointed.* That's when people enter a long-term depression, possibly a lifelong depression.

Many people sadly bought into the lie as a child, which creates a much sturdier set of lies and unrealistic expectations. And no, I'm not blaming everyone's mother for the negative views we adopt. If I do that, I'd be giving my own children an excuse to dump all over mother for all of their problems! I'm a little too savvy for that! I'm also a little too realistic for that.

But the truth is that the lie we plug into the brain at a young age, which often eventually creates an unrealistic expectation, simply has more time to establish itself into our "normal" thought patterns, making it all we know about any given matter. That lie might be all we've practiced for 20 or 30 years.

Example: The child in the second grade who notices that the teacher always calls on the prettiest girl in the room first. Unrealistic expectation: I will be successful and gain attention as long as I'm attractive.

Example: The young boy who's learned the way of the "fuzz buster," which is a simple device placed on the car dashboard. It warns the driver if the police are using radar in the area to catch speeders who are *breaking the law.* Unrealistic expectation: Since it's okay for Mom and Dad to *break the law* or the *rules* as long as they don't get caught, then it must be okay for me to break the rules (law) as well, as long as I don't get caught.

In both of these cases, life might throw these children some real curve balls! Our little girl might spend a lifetime frustrated because her attempts at beauty aren't producing the results of success and attention that she *unrealistically expects* she should have. And our young man might sadly experience the *truth* that it's not okay to break the law, because you don't necessarily get away with it, and such an *unrealistic* belief might complicate and alter the rest of his life.

The first time I observed this principle was while I was a very young woman, probably a teenager. I was watching some afternoon talk show at my parents' home, and the host was interviewing Miss Texas. Anyone who knows anything about Texas knows that more than many other states, they value feminine beauty. I would guess that many a pageant winner had her roots in Texas. As this woman was being interviewed, I couldn't help but be envious of her stunning beauty and poise, to say nothing of her talent and smarts.

As the interview continued, I was thinking about how many women in America would kill to be her! Apparently, the interviewer had the same thoughts, because he then asked her, "What is it like to be Miss Texas, so beautiful and talented? Wow, guys must just be in line for you to give them a look, or even better your phone number." She got quiet, looked at him, and stated, "Yes, but I didn't exactly make it to Miss America, did I?"

Ouch! I can remember being so confused by her comment. How many women would do anything to achieve even half of what she had accomplished as well as have half of the natural beauty she had been blessed with, but what was her expectation? Apparently, Miss America was her goal, her *expectation*. If that was her "Perfect 10," her unrealistic expectation, then do you realize that while she achieved a score of 9.9 in the eyes of almost all people in this world, she was still disappointed and unhappy with the outcome?

The difference between the *unrealistic expectation* variety of lie and the straight-out *falsehood* variety of lie is that the unrealistic expectation begins with the *hint* of truth, the carrot of possibility. We then begin to attach our own beliefs or desires to that *hint* of truth, and we create our own *new* truth, which is nothing more than an *unrealistic expectation*, which sets us up for disappointment and depression.

Example: A child is never reprimanded or given consequences for his lack of responsibility at home but is always given a "kids will be kids," accompanied by a smile from mother. This child begins to believe that he can skirt work and still be applauded by his family and authorities. *Unrealistic!*

The hint of truth lies in the fact that it *was* the truth with his mother. The *lie* is simply the belief that others will love or coddle him as his mother did regardless of whether or not he does his work. If this person buys into the *lie*, he will more than likely spend much of his adulthood griping or complaining about how his boss or spouse has it in for him, is giving him more work than he gives to the other employees, or is always nagging him about the work he "hasn't been able" to finish rather than acknowledging that he hasn't done the required task at his job or at home without repeated reminders. This person's *expectation* of work and responsibility is *unrealistic* and will plague or complicate his life and relationships for years to come if he doesn't get on board with the *truth.*

Example: The Christmas holidays are approaching for a wife and mother of three, but this mother begins to slump into a depression. For years, she felt she organized the *perfect* Christmas for the entire family. That is *unrealistic* as well as misguided! The hint of truth is that she was able to pull it off superficially for several years and believed she had orchestrated the perfect Christmas. But almost a year ago, she discovered that her husband had been having an affair. While she still loves her husband, has worked through counseling with him, and has seen him repent and watched him do all he can do to be accountable, she can't help but feel that the perfect Christmas will never again be possible for her.

The *lie* is, what does this difficult relationship issue, which still needs years of healing and work, have to do with the celebration of the birth of Christ? The *lie* is that Christmas represented the perfect Norman Rockwell picture—with all family members smiling, no children screaming, the perfect amount of snow falling—rather than a nor'easter that shut off the electricity, etc. The *truth* needed to pull her out of the depression is for her to ask herself whether she should get her Christmas marching orders from Norman Rockwell or from the Lord.

WHOSE TRUTH SHOULD WE LISTEN TO ANYWAY?

Unfortunately, when individuals create their own *truth* or *expectation* of what life should look like, logic would dictate that they're on a collision course with the God's reality, God's *truth*, because only *He* represents total *truth*. When our truth butts heads with God's *truth*, guess who wins? Guess who's right? It's that moment of disappointment that sets us up for the loss we then experience, leaving us angry, frustrated, and depressed. How much more logical and simple life can be when we just get on board with His *truth* and leave *our expectations* at the door?

Let's look at another example of this principle. Take the young entrepreneur who enters my office. He had told himself, and fully believed, that he could make his first million dollars by his 25th birthday. While this is possible, it is very *unrealistic*. It would be far more realistic if he made this a lifelong goal and then worked very hard to achieve it early. As he nears his 28th birthday, he has made a substantial amount of money, far more than most young men his age. Yet he comes in frustrated and depressed because he has been unable to achieve what *he* was certain *he* could accomplish. In his mind, that accomplishment was *his* own *truth*, and now he's a failure! The depressed person sets for himself an *unrealistic goal*, a *truth* of *his* own, and then he becomes disappointed when he's unable to achieve it.

SATAN'S MODUS OPERANDI

Have you noticed how similar this *expectation* method for discontentedness is to the way satan operates? As a brief side note, let's look at the brilliance of the use of *unrealistic expectations* to discourage, depress, and incapacitate the average person as opposed to using the flat-out lie. And this is why, my friend, it's a tool used so often by the deceiver himself. Most of us can recognize the flat-out lie pretty quickly and will therefore toss it out of our schema, schema being the screening and evaluating process we all go through with every thought.

Satan does not begin by blasting us with the obvious lie, as we pointed out earlier. He begins by whispering in our ears what we *should* have in life, what we *deserve* for being such good people, for being such hard workers, for being honest or moral when others around us are not. Then he begins to build on *our expectations* of what *we* think we *should* have and couples it with *our* worldly desires.

Example: "With your righteous lifestyle, I would have thought the godly people in your church would have better recognized your many talents. Certainly God recognizes them, but I wonder why He hasn't chosen to reward you in some greater way, more in alignment with your high standing with fellow parishioners and especially considering all the money and time you give to the church."

Example: "With your incredible work ethic, shouldn't God have given you that promotion at work? Instead, He gave it to the guy who sneaks out early whenever the boss leaves early. I thought God was fairer than that. Do you think He just had more important things to oversee that day? Or perhaps He's not really sovereign over the less important things of life."

Example: "You have been so moral in your single life when so many of your friends, even your Christian friends, have been promiscuous. I would think that God would have brought you a Christian boyfriend by now. Perhaps He has one in the future, but for now He certainly wouldn't expect you to never even date or get out once in a while, even if it means temporarily dating a non-Christian."

Each scenario sets us up for feelings of *discontentedness, disappointment,* and *unhappiness* with our current state, which causes us to question God's love and sovereignty. "If He really loved me and is sovereign as my pastor says He is, wouldn't *God* have...?" You can fill in any expectation you have in your own life. Most of us have at least one or two tucked away in our minds and hearts.

THE FLAT-OUT LIE

Example: The flat-out lie would state, *"My father doesn't love me."* We all know that's probably a ridiculous statement, so we eliminate it. But when we begin to entertain a thought that carries the *hint* of *truth,* the *carrot* of *possibility,* and then begin to spin and create our own *truth,* we're on our way to creating lies that lead to *unrealistic expectations.*

For example, if a child says to herself, "Well I know my father loves me, but if he really loved me wouldn't he want to spend more time with me? Wouldn't he have stayed with Mom and me, and tried a little harder to work on the marriage so we could stay together? He certainly spends plenty of time with his new girlfriend. Does he love her more than me? Does he even want to spend time with me, or is he only thinking about her when he's with me? Maybe he doesn't really love me but only shows up to see me because it makes him look like a good father. Maybe if I were as pretty or as smart as his girlfriend, Dad would love me more. Maybe if Dad broke up with her, he would have more time for me and would love me more. Maybe if I could get him and Mom back together, he would spend time with me again and I would be certain of his love. He probably just doesn't really love me. Perhaps *I'm* just not loveable."

Ouch! Do you see the possible myriad of confused messages one spins in the mind when building on that hint of possibility? This little girl might begin to create *unrealistic expectations* of what a father's love *should* look like in her mind, of what she *should* look like to capture Dad's heart, eventually transferring that thought to what she *should* look like to capture any man's heart. (We're experiencing a record number of plastic surgeries among teens today, specifically breast enhancements. Has anyone done a study to compare the number of such surgeries to the number of little girls who don't feel unconditionally loved? It might surprise us.)

Not only could this little girl begin to develop *unrealistic expectations* about her appearance and desirability to the opposite sex, but if she begins to believe all this spin, she might begin to believe that the multiple relationships we all enjoy in life—family, friends, co-workers, etc.—are simply a manifestation of a person's lack of love for the other party (i.e., "Dad can't love me and his girlfriend at the same time. It has to be me or her.").

WHEN UNREALISTIC EXPECTATIONS LEAD TO THE NEED TO CONTROL

This little girl could also begin to entertain the belief that if she could *control* Dad's choices, she could ultimately fix her own pain, have Dad love her unconditionally, and even help Dad to make better decisions in his own life! How noble! Do you see how belief in this slippery slope of *lying* to ourselves could even empower us to view control as a *positive* in our lives and the lives of others? Eventually, when we practice a behavior long enough, it becomes *normal* to us. It simply becomes our way of life! But sadly, it plays havoc with us when it doesn't work in our lives and our relationships with others.

I had a couple in my office with marriage problems. Not only was their marriage on the brink of divorce, but Mom was also in a state of depression because she believed her children, two girls and a boy, all wanted to live with Dad rather than her. After several sessions I found that Mom was an absolute *control freak*! One day I confronted Mom with the question, "What has you so *afraid* that you have the need to control everyone in your life?"

In tears, she began to share that she had been married once before at the young age of 21. She was thrilled to get pregnant at 23, but shortly after this wonderful news, her husband was diagnosed with a rare form of cancer. The stress on her caused her to have a miscarriage, and her husband died shortly afterward. She began to believe and rehearse that if she could have *controlled* the situation, everything would have turned out all right. That was totally *unrealistic*. She has no power over life and death! But as she began to derive *peace* in controlling little things in her life, *controlling* took on a life of its own, leading her to almost blow up her marriage and relationship with her children. Her breakthrough came as she realized how *unrealistic* it was to believe her control could really create the *perfect* life. Quite the opposite—it created *havoc!*

Not only can controlling others become a rehearsed message, but look at how it also so clearly appeals to the human heart. It feeds our *pride.* Pride, I believe, is the origin of all man's worldly sins. This *unrealistic expectation* that controlling others' decisions will fix life's problems is rampant. It is the underlying factor behind most of our control issues. Once we begin to enter the world of controlling others, we open the floodgates to prideful relationship problems from arguments with spouses, children, parents, siblings, co-workers etc.:

> *What causes fights and quarrels among you? Don't they come from your desires that battle within you? You want something but don't get it. You kill and covet, but you cannot have what you want. You quarrel and fight...* (James 4:1-2).

Example: We must control what our spouse wears. We must control what sports *we* feel our children should participate in rather than what they enjoy most. We must control where the extended family vacation will take place each year. We know the most efficient method to achieve higher sales, even though we have a manager who was hired for that specific purpose.

THE TRUTH ABOUT CONTROL

"The Lord does whatever pleases Him, in the heavens and on the earth, in the seas and all their depths" (Ps. 135:6).

The truth is that He is in control! It is our *unrealistic expectations* that confuse and complicate our lives.

The number of people entering my office wanting and needing to *control* others or circumstances is very high. They unrealistically believe it is not only possible to control others, but that it is also beneficial to all. This myriad of unrealistic beliefs, because they are based on lies, sets us up for a future of *frustration* and *disappointment* when our control doesn't work. This leads to *depression* rather than finding contentment and rest in God's *sovereignty* and *unconditional* love.

THE ONE TO TEN VIEW OF LIFE

One of the first places I try to take my depressed clients is to get them back on board with realistic expectations rather than unrealistic ones. I do this by using my one to ten *view* of life, one being the bottom of the barrel and ten representing perfection. Depressed people usually have their eye on the ten, and then are regularly disappointed when life dishes out something below their expectations. And do you realize that if you're looking for that perfect ten, even a 9.9, something most of us would be thrilled with, actually becomes a moment of letdown or disappointment. Remember our Texas beauty queen?

While many depressed people would be quick to point out that they're hardly looking for a perfect ten, (perhaps you are doing that very thing right now), what we must realize is that because we create our own *truth*, we are in charge of creating our own perfect ten. For example, one young man's perfect ten would be to find a woman suited to him with brains, beauty, a desire to succeed in life, and a desire to have at least 2.4 children. Another young man's perfect ten might be to simply find a woman who would agree to marry him and cook at least three days a week! The issue is not that some mystical formula constitutes the perfect ten, but the fact that when you create your own ten, you've just set yourself up with an unrealistic expectation, as you have no knowledge what life or God has around the corner for you.

I just had a young woman in my office state that she fully expects to live until she's at least 125 because she lives such a healthy lifestyle. I started to laugh until I realized I was the only one laughing. She was serious! I eventually asked her how that fit in with the *truth* of Psalm 139:16 where God tells us that *"all the days ordained for me were written in Your book before one of them came to be,"* and unfortunately, God doesn't give us the scoop up on when our individual time is up.

While the realization that the date of our birth and death are already determined by God shouldn't cause us to quit eating our vegetables, exercising, or driving with our seat belt on at all times, it should help us to grasp the realistic expectation that we have no clue if we even have another tomorrow, much less another 100 years. How difficult it would be for this young woman to face a life-threatening disease. What a surprise that she was not familiar with the passage. How calming for me to realize that I don't have to create new *truths* for myself or my clients, as *God's* Word never changes.

ONE TO TEN EXAMPLES

A ten might be the day a bride walks down the aisle with all the hopes and dreams of an excited child. A one might be the day she finds her love of 20 years has committed adultery. A ten might be the day you hit the lottery! A one might be the day you file for bankruptcy. A ten might be the day you bring that first baby home from the hospital. A one might be the day you get that dreaded phone call from the police that your child has been in a fatal car crash. The *truth* is that as hard as we try in life to have fulfillment in our relationships, success in our finances, and protection for our loved ones, problems abound not only due to sin but also because that's simply a condition of life, which usually causes life to average out at about a *realistic five.*

Jesus Himself stated in Matthew 5:45, *"He causes His sun to rise on the evil and the good, and sends rain on the righteous and the unrighteous."* In other words, both garbage and blessing land on every one of us!

Sadly, depressed people are continually looking for their perfect ten and always living a life of disappointment because *it doesn't exist on earth.* I always tell my clients that if they're stuck on finding that elusive *perfect* ten, they better also make arrangements with the undertaker, as it only exists in *Heaven.* And if you think you've found that elusive ten, don't blink because it will vanish as fast as it arrived.

Does this sound cynical? I hope it sounds *realistic.* Christians often fall into this disappointed group, as many of them believe they should receive some kind of special privilege or blessing from God, and if they don't receive those special favors from God, He must either be punishing them, or perhaps He's favoring someone else over them, etc. Did they not read the entire Bible? Or perhaps they only read the parts that fit their desires or fulfill their high expectations.

A young wife and mother is so depressed she's entertained suicidal thoughts. Her husband's income has dropped dramatically during the economic downturn, and she doesn't understand why God doesn't help *his* sales to increase because, after all, her husband is a fine Christian man. The *truth* is that if God increased the sales figures for all Christians, who wouldn't be a Christian just for the perks? That's not why God wants us to choose Him. The *truth* is that God loves to give us the perks that *He has* promised us. They might include a *"peace...which transcends all understanding"* (Phil. 4:7) while we're going through those ravaging economic downturns, making us a blessing to others as well as a Christian who glorifies God.

When we're scanning life's circumstances, looking at all events through the eyes of a one to ten, *realistic* eyes soon realize that life generally averages out to a five. Most brides soon learn after the honeymoon that their knight is actually flawed. This certainly does not mean that all husbands commit adultery. But do some forget repeatedly to take out the garbage? Do some forget to call if they're going to be home late from work? Do some wives, when in the middle of a fight, always dredge up the old mistakes their husbands made? Do some wives direct their husbands' driving while on the road? These are all fives! Expect them. Learn how best to work with them. But certainly, don't be let down by them, as if your husband or wife could rid themselves of annoying or sinful behaviors. If we could make ourselves perfect, what did Christ need to come to this earth for anyway?

ANNOYING SPOUSES

So many couples come to my office complaining that even though they've repeatedly explained to their spouse their annoyance with a particular behavior, their spouse continues to do the behavior, as if they do the behavior to purposely aggravate them. How egocentric.

Most of us do annoying behaviors simply because we're imperfect. We should all be categorized as a five. I regularly tell my clients that my husband and I are the happiest married couple that we know. Why? Hardly because we're perfect. It's because we look for a five in each other, and my sweet husband never performs as a five. He's almost always at least a seven or eight, which always greatly exceeds my expectations, making me regularly thrilled with him. If he has an anger outburst, he might be a three. When my sarcasm rises to my not totally tamed tongue, I probably score a three as well. But when we get away for a weekend with good food, good intimacy, and lots of laughs, we probably both score about a 9.5! If we're expecting Mr. or Mrs. Perfect, expect to be regularly disappointed. But when we are realistic in our expectations, we're not thrown for a loop when our spouse exhibits what will inevitably reveal sin in the form of selfishness, pride, rudeness, etc.

For over 30 years I've had the nasty habit of leaving all my kitchen cabinets open. My husband and all of my children have taken turns slowly closing one cabinet after another while giving me a broad grin. Even my 3-year-old granddaughter looked around my kitchen one day, stating, "Grandma, you silly, why are your cabinets all open?" She then went around methodically closing them one at a time, to my embarrassment. And even though I could have impaled my husband with the open cabinet door time and again, he doesn't care about the cabinets. I don't leave them open on purpose, I apologize, but unfortunately, I do it over and over again. My kitchen, however, is always squeaky clean—presto, I just achieved a five! So stop the presses, realize there are no perfect tens this side of Heaven, and begin to enjoy people where they are, as they are, looking for them to perform as a nice, normal five, and you might even be pleasantly surprised to see yourself and others perform at a much higher score than expected, providing you're looking for that five.

MOVE FROM YOUR HEART
TO YOUR BRAIN

When I first work with clients to use the one to ten *view* of *life*, I urge them to move from their heart to their brain. Why? Because we are reminded in Jeremiah 17:9, *"The heart is deceitful above all things and beyond cure. Who can understand it?"* The heart reflects our desires and feelings rather than the truths of life and of God. Our heart flutters high and low depending on which way the wind blows and the crow flies. God's Word is *stable*; just like God, His Word never changes.

John 1:1 states, *"In the beginning was the Word, and the Word was with God, and the Word was God."*

We need to get to the brain because our feelings are totally untrustworthy. Let's face it, ladies, if women ever allowed their feelings to rule over their choices and beliefs, once a month, during that nasty week most women experience, we would certainly divorce our husbands, sell our children, burn down our houses, change our hair color, and regret it all a week later!

LIFE'S INSTRUCTION MANUAL

The only way for us to go from the heart to the brain is to logically read *life's instruction manual*, the Bible, where *all* truth for life and its problems exists. I have not yet had one problem enter my office that doesn't have the resolution buried somewhere in the *principles* of that greatest book. Ironically, while I mostly have a Christian practice, I also have many Jewish, Moslem, and agnostic clients seeking help for problems. Oh, what a shock that the principles used for the Christian work also work well for the non-Christian. Since God created people, is it not logical to go to the Creator to fix problems rather than rely on humankind's *psychobabble* answers, better known as *whispered lies*? Would I take a broken watch to an auto mechanic for repair or to the creator of the watch? Whatever the religion, God still made the product. He knows how it works and how best to fix it.

Years ago, when my husband and I were newlyweds, we bought our first grill. I don't recall that we had much in the way of furniture, but we had to have a grill so we could cook on our little ten by four apartment porch. Well, being the brilliant and recent college graduates that we were, we could see the main parts of the grill and decided to simply put the grill together without the benefit of the lengthy directions, which to this day we both detest reading. Any guess concerning the final product? We ended up with a huge pile of leftover screws, and if there was any breeze, or if we blew really hard on it, the grill would sway in the breeze!

I wish I could say that we learned our lesson and henceforth always followed the directions, resulting in a superior product. Unfortunately, our sin nature persists in living that old Frank Sinatra lyric, "I did it my way." Then we wonder why life is out of control wobbly and we're left with a coffee tin filled with extra screws. God gave us an incredible instruction manual for life and all relationships, *His Word.* The only problem is that no one wants to read the manual. It's God's decrees, the truths of His Word that we must adhere to in difficult times. Several verses from Psalm 119 most eloquently address this principle:

> *Your word, O Lord, is eternal; it stands firm in the heavens* (Psalm 119:89).

> *Your word is a lamp to my feet and a light for my path* (Psalm 119:105).

> *Your statutes are wonderful; therefore I obey them* (Psalm 119:129).

> *Great peace have they who love Your law* [probably one of the number-one problems for those who come to a counselor—lack of peace!] (Psalm 119:165).

THE NEXT STEP: COGNITIVE BEHAVIORAL THERAPY (PHILIPPIANS 4:8)

Once I work with clients, helping them to see the importance of filling their brain with *realistic expectations* using alignment to God's Word as their barometer, rather than the *unrealistic lies* we choose to believe, we then go to the psychology model that has had increasing success in the treatment of depression, *cognitive behavioral therapy.*[4] Your cognitions are your thoughts, your thoughts affect your feelings, your feelings affect your physical sensations and your physical sensations affect your behavior. The result is a "therapy" or a wellness[5] (see figure 1). I can remember first learning about this form of therapy in graduate school and suddenly realizing that it was actually in alignment with the Bible.

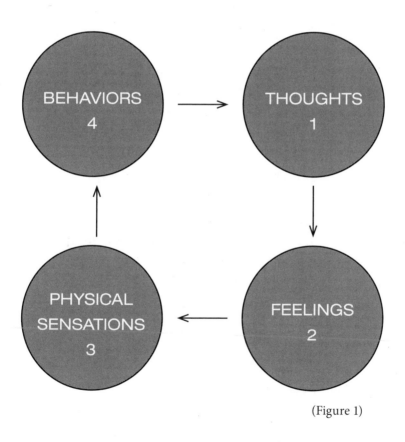

(Figure 1)

Philippians 4:8-9 states:

> *Finally, brothers, whatever is true, whatever is noble, whatever is right, whatever is pure, whatever is lovely, whatever is admirable—if anything is excellent or praiseworthy—think about such things...put it into practice. And the God of peace will be with you.*

What a shock that a method for mental wellness actually came first from the Bible written thousands of years ago, a method that has been counterfeited by humankind for centuries! *Humanity's method* for mental wellness would be labeled *positive thinking.*

But there is a distinct difference in *humanity's* and *God's* method for wellness. God's method for wellness begins with *truth, God's truth,* which never changes. *"Finally, brothers, whatever is **true**"* (Phil. 4:8). However, humanity's method for wellness begins with *a person's own truth,* which only aligns with the positives that make them feel good— at that moment, in that particular year, in that particular culture, in that specific family system, etc. Can you see that word *psychobabble* rear its ugly head?

Can we even count the number of books written and expensive seminars taught about the benefits of *positive thinking* as it relates to depression, anxiety, fulfillment in life, business ventures, maximizing your potential, and achieving untold riches, just to name a few? But the *truth* is that God wrote about this kind of thinking long before humankind's version, but God begins with the most important element of all: *realistic truth* rather than *unrealistic lies!* This is what distinguishes God's plan for wellness from *humanity's* desperate attempts to counterfeit God's original plan for *peace.*

God bases His positive thinking process on *truth first.* Notice the first word in Philippians 4:8 is an instruction to meditate on what is *true.* This is because if the positive thinking is not based on truth, it is only each person's individual truth, which can change by the minute, by the day, and by the year, rendering that positive thinking to the empty and shallow psychobabble that it is, because it is not rooted in the truth that never changes. It becomes nothing more than humankind's superficial self-help. Only when the positive thoughts align with *truth* can they work to give the mind real clarity and relief.

OUR DIRTY LITTLE WOUND

Fraud in our thinking is like putting a Band-Aid on a dirty wound. It covers up the problem temporarily, but an infection is continuing to fester unseen. Infection left untreated will eventually poison the entire body. Likewise, beliefs that are *untrue*—often *unrealistic*, when given the status and privileges of *truth* in one's life—also have the potential to poison the mind and eventually poison the person's life.

Example: A depressed mother of three has a husband who has chosen to divorce her because "he just doesn't feel the connection any longer." She has been trying to apply positive thinking to her circumstances but still can't shake feelings of fear and sadness. She's been telling herself that God will find her a new, better husband who will love her unconditionally, as she had hoped would be the case with her first husband. She's been telling herself that she'll find a new job that will fit into a schedule that will accommodate her and her children. "God can do anything He wants, and I certainly think He has that perfect job out there." She's been telling herself that her husband will eventually realize his mistake and want her back, but by then it will be too late because she will have moved on to greener pastures.

NOW WHAT'S THE TRUTH

Now that's what humankind's *psychobabble* positive thinking could logically conclude. The problem we have, however, is that none of what she is telling herself has any basis in truth. That's not to say her positive thoughts couldn't happen, but it is to say that God never promised any of these things, so she's only meditating on things she would like to happen. Sadly, somewhere in that deeper part of her brain that sifts out fact from fiction, she knows her statements are desires rather than truth. Sadly, she's trying to buy into the less-painful lie, thinking that will assuage her pain. She wants to buy into the *unrealistic expectation* of what she believes God should do for her, of what she feels she deserves in life, and of what she believes is "noble, right, pure, lovely, admirable, excellent, and praiseworthy;" but if her noble, right, pure, lovely, admirable, excellent, and praiseworthy thoughts are built on lies, then of course they will fall down around her; it's just a matter of time.

What will happen to this woman if she finds no desirable man who would even think of marrying a woman with three children still at home with her? What will happen to this woman if she is just too exhausted to even think about dating now that the added responsibilities of being a single mom overwhelm her? What will happen to this woman when she remembers how certain she was that her first husband would never leave her "till death do us part"? Was she deceived by him? Why would she know better what to look for the second time around when she was so mislead by her first husband?

And what will happen to this woman if the excellent job she had 15 years ago with flexible hours and an excellent pay scale is no longer available to her since she's been out of the work place for so many years? What will happen to this woman's heart if her husband suddenly announces he is going to remarry a woman ten years her junior, and he wants the children to be a part of the wedding ceremony? If our thoughts aren't based on truth first, if they're based on lies, then it's inevitable the next generation of thoughts will exhibit those same lies setting us up for *unrealistic expectations* and certain *disappointment*, which leads to *depression.*

The *truth* is that only God Himself is certain to never leave us or forsake us, not only because He said it, but also because God has *never* lied; He can't lie. The truth is that God never said He would find this woman a new husband. The truth is that her husband has been given a free will to choose to obey God or to sin. There are no guarantees he will suddenly decide to obey God and return to his wife. The truth is that it is very possible her ex-husband will remarry.

NOW LET'S REBUILD ON THE FOUNDATION OF TRUTH

Now that we've looked truth straight in the eye, as painful as that might be, it's time to begin to build on the thoughts that are *noble, right, pure, lovely, admirable, excellent,* and *praiseworthy.* We can begin to meditate on how noble and right it is that God never leaves us. In the middle of the night when we might wake up with that pit of disbelief in our stomach, God is there to comfort us. I can call out His name whatever the hour. He's there for you. When our eyes fill with tears looking at a family photo, we can praise Him for giving us the wonderful blessing of those three children, even though the marriage ended sadly. We can admire Him for His excellent plan of marriage where two become one and then ask Him to help us to remain content until, or if, He sees fit to open that door again for marriage in the future. He's there with you. He won't leave you. That is certainly praiseworthy.

We can meditate on the fact that while God never promised you that perfect job, He deserves to be praised simply for allowing you to be born into a country that gives women the opportunity to get a good education, as well as a good job, that allows women to own property, and that has provisions in the courts that will see to it that women and their children are provided for by an ex-husband. While divorce does not always seem fair, there are many countries where women would be mere castaways at the mercy of corrupt courts or even no courts!

Praise God for His lovely provision of a possible extended family that will be there to help you through this difficult time with emotional support, babysitting help, or financial help. And we can praise God that we have a church family who will reach out to us in our time of need if we let them know we're hurting. We can praise God that His people are His very own hands and feet here to minister to us. Perfectly? No; but lovingly, yes. We can meditate on the truth that He reveals to us in Psalm 34:18, *"The Lord is close to the brokenhearted,"* and in Psalm 147:3 He *"heals the brokenhearted."*

While we can't possibly sort out or immediately deal with all the pain, confusion, or choices made in this tragedy, we can certainly praise Him for the knowledge that His lovely, gentle Spirit will walk us through each long day, working to restore us to healing and abundance. Now those are truths you can take to the bank!

CONNECTING COGNITIVE BEHAVIORAL THERAPY WITH PHILIPPIANS 4:8

The basis for cognitive behavioral therapy is that your *thoughts* birth your *feelings,* your *feelings* affect your *physical sensations,* and your *physical sensations* affect your *behavior.* That cycle occurs in the brain approximately 10,000 times each day (for those of us who are a bit OCD, I suspect we process about 12,000 thoughts per day!),[6] but needless to say, our conscious brain only catches or recognizes a fraction of those thoughts. This accounts for why people so often state that they suddenly "felt" sad or lonely but don't know why they felt a particular feeling, as they can't recall any thought that preceded the feeling.

Often people wake up in the morning stating they feel blue or exhausted. This is because the brain is one of the organs in the body that never stops, even while we're sleeping. Consequently, we might be processing sad or depressing thoughts all night, or we might be wrestling with problems in our sleep and will logically wake up sad or tired simply because the cognitive process never quits; our thoughts (perhaps thinking about the loneliness of a relationship breakup) birth our *feelings* (probably sad), our feelings affect our *physical sensations* (sad thoughts produce a lethargic body), and the physical sensations affect our *behavior* (waking up blue and still exhausted).

Let's look at how this aligns itself with Philippians 4:8. God tells us to meditate on things that are first of all true, then noble, right, pure, lovely, admirable, excellent, and praiseworthy. He then tells us to put this into practice and *"the God of peace will be with you."* So essentially, God is telling us to *pull* the *well* thoughts out of *truthful* circumstances, meditate on those *well* thoughts, and you will achieve peace in your lives.

Two thousand years later *science* tells us that what we meditate on is the key to the way we feel. *Science* tells us that if we meditate on sad thoughts, we will be sad and our bodies and behaviors will reflect sadness. *Science* tells us that if we meditate on angry thoughts, we will be angry people and our bodies and behaviors will reflect anger. *Science* tells us that if we meditate on well thoughts, we will feel well and our bodies and behaviors will reflect well.

SCIENCE GETS US HALFWAY THERE

Science is correct in these teachings, as they are simply an imitation of the principle put forth in Philippians 4:8 with *one snag.* Science can only get us halfway there, because science and human's application of these science-only principles (i.e., psychobabble) doesn't begin with truth, and without truth as the foundation, peace can't possibly be achieved. As we pointed out on page one, the superficial and the shallow just don't cut it for humankind in the long haul; building thoughts on the superficial, on the untrue, would be akin to building a house on a sandy foundation. There is in all of humankind a longing for *truth*, for a deeper understanding of why we experience the pain and the heartbreaking circumstances that appear so unfair or confusing and that eventually affect every human being. Man aches for true resolve to difficulty.

The application of *psychobabble* or superficial methods to resolve these difficulties will only create a *battleground* in the heart and mind— one part of the heart and mind logically wanting a quick fix for our pain and questions, the other part of the heart and mind longing for those deeper understandings and healings that will stand the test of time as well as stand the "level" of hurt that the enemy will sling at us. The psychobabble answer creates a battleground because the *shallow, superficial* answers simply don't resonate in the brain. And what do battlegrounds produce? They produce war, death, impoverishment, sadness, confusion, disappointment, depression, and yes, war usually produces a winner and a loser. And the pride in the heart of humanity causes a person to continue in an endless fight to the death rather than lose. (That's really peaceful.)

These are only some of the outward symptoms manifested when the war rages within the heart. As long as a battle is being waged in the mind and heart, these symptoms will dominate. Why? Because your *thoughts* birth your *feelings*, your feelings affect your *physical sensations,* and your physical sensations affect your *behavior*. And the cycle continues!

SYMPTOMS OF THE
RAGING WAR WITHIN

People come into my office because they are manifesting the symptoms of a raging war within themselves. They desperately want peace, an end to the war that is raging. That *war* keeps them up at night and causes them to be only a blink away from tears or anger more moments of their day than not; it causes havoc and confusion in their daily relationships. That war keeps them in a constant state of discontentedness, and while that state tremendously increases shopping sales at the malls and beer sales at the local pubs, it also rips at their souls, attacks their bodies physically, and robs them of their *peace*. It's only with those deeper understandings that we can have real peace—the peace that endures, the peace that is not getting its direction from only circumstances or quick fixes, and the peace that makes no earthly sense!

Most of us would acknowledge that the way we *feel* is actually a barometer of how we would describe the quality of our lives. The way we feel, like it or not, will affect many of our behaviors, ultimately most of our future choices. When we *feel* at *peace* in most any situation, we would generally describe our life as satisfying, as happy. Notice that description of one's life doesn't come from a description of our *circumstances*. It comes from a description of our *state of mind* in the circumstances.

God states in John that He wants us to have an abundant life and then lays out instructions in His manual, the Bible, specifically Philippians 4:8, as to a key ingredient needed to attain that life. Science alone gives us the quick fix for wellness, the CliffsNotes' version, the psychobabble method, which is a cheap version of God's total wellness program. Humanity's methods want to eliminate the most important component to wellness, the key ingredient that makes the entire process work: *truth*. Why? Because by acknowledging that a *truth* really does exist, we are clearly forced to acknowledge that there is one above humankind, that humanity is not the top of the food chain, and that there could be a God above us all. That's a belief that science and humanity generally don't want to adopt. God's method for wellness demands that all *positive thinking* originates with truth, because without truth as the cornerstone, employing humanity's positive thinking will inevitably result in a chasing of the wind, a total frustration.

QUESTIONS

1) Have you or a family member ever suffered from depression? Would you consider it a severe, mild, or moderate depression?

2) Would you be willing to share what issue triggered that depression?

3) Can you see how an unrealistic expectation of life, what you feel you deserve, what others tell you you deserve, etc., might have actually triggered a disappointment which led to a depression? Can you describe the possible slippery slope from a disappointment to a depression? How and who fed the disappointment which led to the depression?

4) Can you explain in your own words the link between a rehearsed belief for 10-20 years (that might be a lie) and depression?

5) Do you think that living in the United States might play a role in our unrealistic expectations? Explain and give examples.

6) Can you share in what ways you might have looked for a ten in your life?

Chapter 3

THE TRUTH ABOUT
DEPRESSION: PART 2

I SIT AND WAIT

And so there I sit, listening to a person's story, waiting to hear those little lies, the psychobabble that the world spins out in record numbers that people have held fast to for a short period of time during a particular problem episode, or for all of their lives. Those *little lies* are whispered in our ears by a loving family member, a friend who just wants us to feel better, or a wounded mind screaming for justice and are meant to give people the world's version of how to feel good in a difficult life riddled with pain and problems. I sit there knowing that unless we can get a person's thinking in alignment with the *truth*, no amount of *positive spin* will relieve them of their depression, their hurt.

For any of you movie buffs out there, a perfect example of how the world's quick-fix methods are meant to relieve pain but how they don't work overall if they're not based on truth, can be found in a movie starring Hugh Grant, released several years ago called *Nine Months*. Hugh Grant had just experienced an ugly breakup with his girlfriend and was complaining about her to his best friend, actor Jeff Goldblum, who played a great comedy part in the movie. As Hugh Grant was bad-mouthing his ex to his friend, played by Jeff Goldblum, his friend also burst into ugly ranting about this girlfriend, thinking this would make his friend feel better and feel more justified with his comments and his choices concerning the break up. Immediately, Hugh Grant stopped walking and starred angrily at his friend declaring, "You're speaking about the woman I love!" Immediately, Jeff Goldblum burst forth with, "And what a fine woman she is!" The truth was that Hugh Grant loved this woman even though he was ripping angry with her. Instant fixes based on a lie don't work or fix anything. Like cream, truth must always rise to the top! Truth can't be denied. God won't allow it.

MY SUPERMARKET MODEL IMPLEMENTING COGNITIVE BEHAVIORAL THERAPY AND PHILIPPIANS 4:8

Let's take a look at an example of how we might implement Philippians 4:8 with cognitive behavioral therapy. I always call this my "supermarket model." Let's suppose I ran into one of my former clients in the supermarket on a Monday. As I addressed her, asked about her family, job etc., I didn't look at her even *one* time but stared over her shoulder during the entire conversation! My client might very likely become irritated and begin to think I'm being extremely rude, which I am. She might begin to run thoughts through her mind like, *Why is she treating me so inappropriately? She was pleasant in her office but now she's just plain* **rude**. *I'm certainly glad I'm no longer seeing her for help. How could she help me? I wouldn't be able to get past this annoying behavior!*

Now, if those were the thoughts that were running through the mind, how would this person be feeling? I suspect angry at my behavior toward her as she felt she was treated unfairly. Remember, your thoughts birth your feelings. Physical sensations? You know how we get when we're angry. We get all tightened up, not at all relaxed, which is reflected in the way we move. And behavior? When we're angry, we're much more apt to bite someone's head off (sadly, often the ones we love most), we're much more apt to yell at the dog, scold the kids, etc. I believe all the road rage we hear about is rarely about the little lady who cut someone off with her car. Road rage is more often about the argument we had with our spouse before we headed off for work, the disagreement we've had with our employer, the bad grade we got on that college term paper, etc. That anger that's been building is suddenly unleashed on the road when a person is behind a two-ton vehicle!

Now let's look at that exact same example on Tuesday. Once again, I'm in the supermarket and along comes my former client. Once again, I begin to chat with her and once again I give her absolutely no eye contact but only look over her shoulder as if she weren't even standing there. But on Tuesday, the former client begins to talk to herself with questions like, *I wonder why she is treating me as if I'm not even in the room? It's as if my former counselor doesn't even see me, as if I'm a nobody to her. She probably hardly even remembers me. Obviously, I didn't make much of an impression on her. I feel as if I'm just invisible to her.*

If those are the thoughts that are running through this person's mind, anyone want to guess how she is feeling about now? If our thoughts birth the way we feel, I would venture a guess that this person is feeling rather sad as all she's been telling herself is how unimportant and insignificant she is. Physical sensations would clearly reflect lethargy and tired and slow movements, and perhaps facial expressions that reflect sadness. This person's behavior would manifest signs of low-grade depression, like tearful or sad responses to otherwise neutral events. Why? Because the thoughts (self-deprecating) birth the feelings (sad) and reflect the physical sensations (body and face begin to reflect sadness), which affects one's behavior (depressed).

Now let's look at Wednesday, and yes, we'll look at the exact same circumstance applying the more truthful aspects of Philippians 4:8, which directs me to begin by meditating on what is *true*. Again, I'm in my favorite supermarket and again I meet a former client. Again, I begin to chat about the day, about how she is doing, about my new dog, etc. Again, I never give them eye contact but look over her shoulder the entire time. However, today the former client focuses her self-talk on *truth*. Just like on Monday and Tuesday, she quickly notices my lack of eye contact. She also begins her self-talk questioning my behavior, but this time the former client begins at the truth by acknowledging that it's *my* behavior, and *my* behavior has nothing to do with her. She might laughingly wonder if her former counselor has been doing a bit too much therapy and is now in some serious *need* of therapy herself. The client might wonder what on earth the former counselor is staring at. *Perhaps there's one gorgeous guy standing behind me, or maybe there's a lady with a dress cut down to her navel, but whatever she's looking at, I'm curious. I want to see what's over there!*

LET'S MEDITATE ON WHAT IS LOGICAL AND TRUTHFUL

Look at how much more *logical* and *truthful* those thoughts are. They are based on the truth that the client has no clue as to why the counselor is looking behind the client instead of giving eye contact. Therefore, the client doesn't randomly conclude *why* the counselor is acting in such a manner, basing their beliefs on his or her own agenda or self-esteem issues. The client might speculate in some lighthearted manner as to what in the world the counselor is doing, but the speculations are not all about herself, nor is the client choosing *a truth* that's all about herself or what she believes about herself (example: "people are always treating me rudely," or "people always treat me as if I'm a nobody," etc.). If the counselor is acting rudely or inattentively, what does that have to do with the client? Isn't that more a reflection of the counselor's poor behavior or character? And why should the counselor's behavior or character affect the mood, responses, or life of the client?

Notice that on Monday, when the client felt angry because she believed the counselor's behavior was rude, the client made the counselor's behavior all about *herself.* And *her* behavior—anger—became a direct result of the thoughts she had about the counselor. And why did the client feel angry? Because your *thoughts* birth your *feelings,* your feelings affect your *physical sensations,* and your physical sensations affect your *behavior.* On Tuesday, when the client felt sad because she believed the counselor was belittling and inattentive to her, the client again made the counselor's behavior all about *herself,* and again the client's behavior—depressed—became a direct result of the thoughts she had about the counselor—*thoughts, feelings, physical sensations, and behavior.*

On each of these days, the client was totally *self-*focused, scanning events in a way that focuses on her own wounded or fragile ego, focusing on how others might have been treating her inappropriately, etc. Essentially, she made another person's behavior all about herself when the truth is that each person's behavior is a reflection of his or her own character or self-interest. Why should anyone think that another person's behavior is about him or her anyway?

IT'S NOT ALL ABOUT YOU

Sadly, people who always make another's behavior about themselves rarely find peace in their lives. Why? Because they're basing their thoughts on a lie, the lie being that life centers on *them* and that people are always reacting to *them.* How unrealistic it is to think that we are really all that important. People who view others' actions in this way are in a constant state of frenzy as they are analyzing and tapping into other people's emotions, moods, circumstances, tone of voice, and body language. Eeek! How exhausting!

Life is hard and busy enough just trying to get through our own day's struggles and activities without owning and reacting to what we *think* others *might* be communicating to us or about us. Making every thought and eventual behavior all about us only fuels our self-centeredness, which leads to that unrealistic disappointment in others, unrealistic disappointment in life, and often an unrealistic disappointment in God.

There's an old Chinese proverb that states, "What the eye sees and the ear hears is already in the heart." Far too often we see, hear, and process in such an egocentric manner that we've lost all sight of truth. Could this be why two people could hear the same speech, see the same movie, and live in the same house, but come away with totally different perspectives?

And how about people who viewed the entire incident at the supermarket with a *truthful* message to their brain, the truth being that they have no clue why their former counselor is looking past them without any eye contact whatsoever? What are this person's thoughts, feelings, physical sensations, and behavior? Is she angry or sad? Not at all. Her thoughts are based on truth (what's up with that counselor?). Her feelings are neutral as she realizes the counselor's behavior has nothing to do with her. Her physical sensations are probably heightened because she is curious as to what is going on behind her. And her behavior is one of jumping into life with two feet, not analyzing everything as if it's all about her, but moving in a forward motion, keeping her eyes on the Lord and His agenda for her life rather than on herself and her constant *self-focus*.

One of my favorite radio pastors, Steve Brown, has shared an expression describing what the Christian life should look like. He states that the Christian life "should be like dancing without looking at your feet." In other words, enjoy the dance! Take your eyes off yourselves. Focus on the Lord and enjoy. That same expression could also apply to our discussion on depression. When we're unrealistically scanning events, making them all about ourselves (looking at our feet), how could we help but become depressed, as all we're doing is focusing on our sinful selves rather than our glorious Lord?

SANDRA'S STORY

Let's look at one more example of how we can connect cognitive behavioral therapy and Philippians 4:8. Lovely young Sandra enters my office with severe depression. She is a Christian wife and a stay-at-home mother of four children. Depending on the level of depression we discuss, possible medication as a *bridge* to wellness, not necessarily as a lifelong choice; however, she's decided she would rather try to work through the depression without medication, especially since she is still nursing her youngest baby. After many tears, she shares the fact that she was sexually molested by an uncle as a young girl. She continues with the all-too-often story of why she didn't tell Mom or Dad. Uncle told her no one would believe her and it would cause so many family problems that the entire family would split up—and yes, only she would be the person everyone would blame.

This abuse occurred for approximately three years, usually when her uncle would babysit her. Several nights each month her father had to stay late at work to do a double shift when someone called in sick at the last minute. Her mother cared for her ailing father three nights each week, a responsibility she shared with a local sister. On the occasions that both Mom and Dad had to be out, Sandra's uncle would come to the house. He always arrived in the early evening just as the sun was setting. Sandra admitted that to this day she fearfully watches as night approaches, insidiously reliving all the horrifying sensations that tormented her mind and body as she would watch the sun set and hear her uncle approach. Sandra recalls crying when her mother left the house, begging Mom to let her go to Granddad's house with her. Mom would simply kiss her goodnight and tell her she needed to remain home so she could "get a good night's sleep."

After several years of abuse, Sandra was finally old enough and able to lock herself in her room when her uncle would come to babysit. She would sit terrified, afraid that her uncle would find a way to get into her room, but eventually the abuse was ended as her uncle realized it was too risky to pursue Sandra any longer. Needless to say, that didn't stop the fear or the nightmares for Sandra. Those have continued. But the client's even greater problem was now the fact that she had never told her husband about the sexual abuse. Years spent with this secret bottled up inside her had led to a severe depression, feelings of low self-esteem, believing she's damaged goods, etc.

We often liken such secrets to holding a beach ball underwater. It continues to get harder and harder to hold down as it takes so much of your time and energy. When it's finally let loose, it shoots up with a vengeance. So her depression and secret had been held underwater and was now surfacing with a vengeance.

Sandra stated that her husband was a fine Christian man. She remembered when they dated she thought he was such a "wonderful catch." He had actually remained sexually pure, wanting to save himself for his bride. She told him he was the only man she had been intimate with but did not include the words "by choice."

"How could he possibly want me if he knew about my horrible past?" she asked. And while she logically realized she was not at fault for the sexual abuse, it had always made her feel dirty, used, and broken. So she stuffed her pain down but continued to view herself as "less than." Sandra felt her depression and guilt had impacted the couple's sex life as well as the way she was raising the children. She had been living a lie for so long, was racked with so much guilt and shame, and now was convinced her husband couldn't possibly forgive her for years of lying. Now she not only saw herself as dirty and used, but as a dreadful liar. I know what every reader is thinking right now. You're thinking her feelings are not *truth*. I totally agree. But *her truth* has become her *reality*.

She had rehearsed her *truth* for so long that she was completely stuck, even sinking in the mire of it.

THE TRUTH MUST SURFACE

Where do we start? With the *truth,* of course, as it *must* come to the surface. But the real truth doesn't begin with the sexual abuse. It begins with the fact that this beautiful girl is a daughter of the living God, the living King. She is precious in His sight. She is a princess. The truth is that when God looks at her, He only sees her purity and loveliness. He values her so much He already died for her so that she can abide with Him for all eternity. The *truth* is that the sad events in Sandra's life will never go away or be erased. That would be a denial of God's Word when He states in Romans 8:28, *"And we know that in all things God works for the good of those who love him, who have been called according to his purpose."* In other words, God wants to make beauty out of ashes.

The truth is that God will be right by her side as she continues to work this out in her life. He will not leave her. The truth is that Sandra's abuse could have led to a life of promiscuity, drugs, etc., but instead she found the love of her life and is now privileged to be married to a Christian husband who loves her, and they have been privileged with four beautiful and healthy children. The truth is that we are living in a fallen world where sin occurs, and while it might take many years for her to work through the sexual abuse, she must realize that a child is unable to control a grown man's actions, and she was completely innocent of any wrong doing. The truth is that the sexual abuse could have lasted far longer, but by God's grace it was stopped before a possible pregnancy or physical violence or even death. But the greater truth in this entire matter is that as long as this young woman focuses on herself, her unworthiness, her abuse, her lies, her justifiable anger, and the unfairness, she will remain in a depression. Why? Because our thoughts (all negative concerning her past and her lies) birth our feelings (sad, hopeless), become our physical sensations (lethargic, no energy, constant pain), and become our behavior (depression).

WHAT IS TRUE...

When we begin to meditate according to Philippians 4:8 on what is *true*, noble, right, pure, lovely, admirable, excellent, and praiseworthy, our thoughts will be filled with what is true: *He helped to pull me out of disaster, away from this evil man's grip, and has blessed me in so many ways.* Our thoughts become our *feelings* (joy and gratitude at what a good God we serve, who has never left me and who will continue to see me through as I share this pain with my husband). They become our physical sensations (renewed energy and appreciation for life and what God wants to do with that life), and our behavior (a Christian walk that is filled with praise and manifests the power of Romans 8:28).

As this young woman began to see real truth, God's truth, she was lifted up, recognizing her beauty in God's eyes, not because of any accomplishments of her own but because He has walked with her every step of the way and will continue to do so. As her eyes are fixed on God, she's not focusing on sin and sadness, but on His glory and greatness, His restoration.

Finally, she was ready to share with her husband, who I realized was the fine Christian man Sandra had described. She had shed so many of the old lies that had warped her mind and was now able to share her past with her husband with the confidence that for certain God would never leave her side. She cried as she revealed her painful past. He wept along with her for all she had gone through and was quick to reassure her of his love for her. How God and Sandra choose to use her in the future is uncertain, but she is fully confident in the truth of Romans 8:28 and now anticipates the future.

QUESTIONS

1) Can you recall a circumstance that was complicated because of the negative thoughts that you allowed in your mind?

2) "What the eye sees and the ear hear hears is already in the mind." What does that say about the person who is continually offended by another person's actions?

3) Where should the focus be in the life of a Christian? How might we set ourselves up for disappointment/depression when our focus is on ourselves or others?

4) The "world's psychobabble" often advocates positive thinking. How might that complicate one's life? How might it make depression worse? Can you recall following such a path?

5) True Christian therapy is aligned with Philippians 4:8. Read the verse and describe how it differs from the world's psychobabble?

Chapter 4

THE TRUTH ABOUT
FAIRNESS

Everyone wants fairness—or do they? This is one of my favorite problems to deal with when people come to my office. Fairness is one of the underlying causes for the depression that so many therapists deal with. It's a problem that of course involves those *little lies* we stack up in our brain that are best buddies with our unrealistic expectations, better known as the world's psychobabble. What is it that people usually see as unfair? People usually begin by viewing life as unfair. They love to throw out the old, "I know life's not fair but..." As soon as they throw out the word *but*, I know they're on the road to wanting that fairness that they just said *doesn't* exist! I know they're on the road to wanting that perfect ten that we all wish for at one time or another.

When we declare that life is unfair, it helps us avoid honing in on specific people we feel have treated us unfairly, it helps us avoid the possessions we haven't received that *we* know we're deserving of. It helps us to deal with the favoritism that the *other* guy always receives, etc., because we realize targeting such specifics only makes us appear jealous or petty. Given enough time, however, the specific targets of the unfairness that people bring to me begin to surface.

THAT'S NOT THE PARENT I WANTED

People are forever angry at their parents because they didn't receive the parent or the treatment from that parent that they feel they deserved or needed. Possibly, their parents treated one or more of their siblings better in some way. Some people never got the "cool parent" they wanted, while others got the parent who was so cool that they were constantly mortified every time "cool Mom" or "cool Dad" opened his or her mouth. Some people "needed" a really nurturing parent, while others got such a nurturing parent that they, to this day, feel totally overwhelmed by the stifling attention. Others wanted the cookie-baking mom, while some feel it unfair that they got the mom who so loved baking those cookies that she never went to her teen's sports events but only stayed at home to bake and was 100 pounds overweight!

Each person sets up his or her *own expectation* of what *fair* should deliver to them and is then let down when their individual *perfect ten* isn't achieved. Are you sensing *unrealistic expectations* in these foolish but often real examples? What's interesting is that we really don't need to go to what most of us would feel is legitimate and deep-wounding unfairness, the alcoholic parent, the physically or sexually abusive parent, etc., to see that unfair thread of *discontent* weaving its way into so many of our thoughts.

While every one of us quotes the statement, *Life's not fair*, we nonetheless whisper to ourselves what life was supposed to deliver to us based on *our* definition of fairness. We *expect* that a fair God will see to it that events will work out in a fair manner, again according to *our* definition of fairness. But what is our definition of *fair*, and who ever said God was fair?

We must begin with a Mr. Webster definition of fair as we view this issue that causes disappointment for so many. *Fair* is defined as "just and honest; impartial, unprejudiced, according to the rules."[1] *Unfair* is defined as "not just or impartial; biased; inequitable."[2] Sounds reasonable so far. But is this actually the way we view fairness, and does God measure fairness with the same barometer that we do? If fair is "according to the rules," whose rules are we using, ours or God's? Does God even value fairness? Is it possible that we might have unrealistic expectations concerning fairness, thereby causing so much frustration and disappointment in our lives?

THE PARABLE OF THE WORKERS

One of the first places we will search for a better understanding of fairness and truth is in the Scriptures. A good starting point is the parable of the workers found in Matthew 20.

> *The workers who were hired about the eleventh hour came and each received a denarius. So when those came who were hired first, they expected to receive more. But each one of them also received a denarius. When they received it, they began to grumble against the landowner. "These men who were hired last worked only one hour," they said, "and you have made them equal to us who have borne the burden of the work and the heat of the day."*
>
> *But he answered one of them, "Friend, I am not being unfair to you. Didn't you agree to work for a denarius? Take your pay and go. I want to give the man who was hired last the same as I gave you. Don't I have the right to do what I want with my own money? Or are you envious because I am generous?"*

So the last will be first, and the first will be last (Matthew 20:9-16).

Bingo folks! I think we've found our first example of how our expectations of fair don't exactly line up with God's truth concerning fair. Did these men get upset because of what they considered an unfair practice? Absolutely! I suspect their expectations of *fair* closely align with what most of us determine as fair. These men had determined what *they* believed *they* deserved based on *their* definition of what fair was. Their definition for fairness became *their* truth, which then became lodged in the brain, but was it God's truth or a lie?

WHO GETS THE NOD?

When our truth doesn't align with God's truth, anyone want to take a stab at who gets the nod? They saw fairness as Mr. Webster declared it with a *pinch* of a lie attached. People believe the lie that *they* should be able to *own, see, experience,* and *live* the *outcome* that they feel they are deserving of or entitled to based on their estimation of what is even and "equitable, without bias, prejudice, or partiality." People desperately want to see their outcome, the fruits of *their* labor, be somehow equal and fair to either what they simply feel they're entitled to, or to what they believe is equal to the effort they believe they have put forth.

Our cry for fairness is very often our prideful hearts believing we deserve what *we* feel is an equal return for *our* efforts, which is often reflected in house, car, and jewelry sales that we can't afford, as well as a cry for a position of notoriety or power that *we* believe we have earned. How often have we been on a school playground only to see a child "cut" in front of another child? This causes the child already in line to yell, "You can't cut in front of me—no fair!" Wanting fairness is ingrained in us from childhood.

It should also be noted that whenever humankind or the enemy attaches a little lie concerning what he or she deserves, who does it puff up, who does it serve, and whose pride is stroked? Ours, of course. *Tweaking* the truth is a far more effective way to cause chaos and confusion than a blatant lie because it completely muddies the waters. It's that little lie that sets us up with the unrealistic expectations that in turn set us up for disappointment and depression.

Therefore, to summarize, the lie originates from either our *pride* or our *works*! Now, does pride or works sound like anything that would originate from God? I hardly think so. Then add to that lie 10, 20, or more years of polishing up the lie, and when truth suddenly or slowly surfaces, as it must in time, when things don't play out according to our scheduled *fair*, the battle between beliefs will begin causing a mental conflict that sets one up for confusion, anger, and depression.

MAN IS A PHYSICAL BEING

Why is humanity's idea of fair so wrapped around tangible outcomes? Notice in the parable of the workers, the workers defined what was fair to them in a totally subjective manner based on *physical* income rather than on the *intrinsic* or *spiritual* returns. Remember, humankind is a physical being. Therefore, we make our evaluations and determinations based on the physical. We look for outcomes in the physical, but God is spiritual. With an understanding of that fact, would God's idea of fairness and outcomes be more likely physical or spiritual? Spiritual, of course. Therein lays our first unrealistic expectation. We want *fair* in the physical when God is trying to speak to us in the spiritual. We're expecting tangible rewards, but that's not necessarily how God might reward or not reward us.

Look at these field workers. They wanted physical fairness as defined by man. Wages based on their effort, their output, or simply what they felt they were entitled to. This is always where people are when they come into my office, although many of them are hesitant to admit it.

And how about that last line in the Matthew passage? *"So the last shall be first, and the first shall be last."* Double ouch! People are continually screaming unfair when it comes to position and money. "If only I had been hired before Sam, he wouldn't have made partner before me. It just doesn't seem fair that he should be making so much more money than I am when there was only one month's difference in our hiring date." "It doesn't seem fair that my roommate gets such a good sports scholarship when I have to work a part-time job just to stay in school." "My brother and I went to the same college, graduated only a year apart, but he took a job out of state, and now he's making so much more than I am. It just doesn't seem fair." "Why is it that my older sister, Susie, can go to the mall without a parent chaperone and Mom won't even discuss when I get to go unsupervised to the mall with my friends?" "Why should I have to suffer with so many headaches? It keeps me from so many of the things I want to do."

If a person begins to plan his or her own pity party based on unfairness, do you realize what 20 or 30 years of rehearsing that broken record can do to a person? Ruts in the brain can go so deep there's often no digging out. Whispered unrealistic expectations about what we are entitled to, what we feel is fair, and what we deserve can become a *way of life,* especially when it has been a *rehearsed* way of thinking. *Practice makes perfect,* and the more we practice a particular way of thinking, the more we create automatic thoughts, which are thoughts that enter the mind as easily and thoughtlessly as breathing.

THE ORIGIN OF THE TEA PARTY MOVEMENT

For those of you who watch CNBC on TV, the financial network, a recent event perfectly illustrates this fairness that so many of us are screaming for. At the time of this writing, this nation, and this world, has been experiencing a frightening financial meltdown. House fore-closures have hit all-time record numbers. Unemployment numbers have been moving toward double-digit numbers. The congress led by our new president has endeavored to resolve the record high unem-ployment rates as well as the record number of national foreclosures by possibly "bailing out" many people who are very close to losing their homes due to nonpayment of their mortgage. Government bailout is meant to aid people by lowering their interest rates and in some cases would even lower their mortgages, making it possible for people to remain in their homes.

The American taxpayer will be picking up the tab for this unprec-edented record deficit. The financial problems have also led to the plummeting of Wall Street stocks and international stock markets as invertors witness lows not seen for many years. One well-known Wall Street commentator suddenly "lost it" on a live morning TV program. To paraphrase his words, this commentator turned to the camera and started yelling out loud. He addressed "Mr. President" and then began to scream about how *unfair* it was that all of us who have been diligently paying our mortgages should have to "bail out" so many of the people who "never should have gotten mortgages in the first place!"

This commenter was so emotional and angry that anyone watch-ing couldn't help but see his level of frustration with a plan that he felt was totally *unfair*. His appearance made such news that clips of his rant were being seen on every newscast for several days. He was the topic of all the financial news programs. He became the new icon hero for all the people nationally who had been vehemently opposed to this expen-sive bailout package, believing it was unfair. It was his comments that actually launched the national Tea Party movement that will no doubt make it into our history books one day. Whatever side of the fence you might have been on, it was a time that about half of the nation was crying unfair! Why did he go so ballistic on live TV, and why did he get such instant notoriety? Because the need for *fairness* resonates in every one of us at some level, to some degree. It screams or it whispers, but it is a universal cry.

COULD GOD BE UNFAIR?

But who is it that we are really calling unfair? If we have a belief in a sovereign God, then we know that the buck stops with Him. We know that He has the power to make anything happen, that He can control any circumstance He wants. If He can part the Red Sea for His children, the Israelites, why can't He save my marriage? If I am one of His children, why won't He save my house from foreclosure, why can't He save my spouse from cancer, why can't He save me from losing my job, why can't He find me a godly husband, why can't He open my womb, and why can't He keep my parents from getting a divorce? We really don't want to come right out and call God unfair, probably for fear of angering Him, so we sneak around, laying our frustrations at the feet of other people, situations, timing, etc. However, each time we are declaring something or someone unfair, we are really saying, "Your sovereignty isn't good, God."

When humankind looks at God's sovereignty, it often makes us very uncomfortable because it's actually in opposition to humanity's idea of fairness. Humanity wants all things fair and equitable based upon works, entitlement, or self-righteousness. If life could be fair based on the human definition for fairness, then humankind would actually be able to have in his or her possession a perfect *formula* for controlling most of his or her own *outcomes,* which would actually put humanity in control rather than God. It would actually have God serving man and woman based on human works rather than humanity serving a sovereign God. It would also give humankind the ability to take the credit for success far more often when life goes well.

God's sovereignty points to the fact that God is in total control of events and that He can do things as He pleases. We want fair to be all about us, all about our works, righteousness, and accomplishments. That's what the workers in the vineyard felt. But that belief doesn't align with humanity's purpose in life, which is to glorify God! The longer the vineyard workers worked, the more they felt they deserved. And when they didn't get what they felt they deserved, they "grumbled." And isn't that actually what we all do at times? We set up *our* own expectations of what we feel we deserve and then grumble when *our* expectations aren't met.

So we know what man and woman's agenda was in the Matthew passage. But what about *God's agenda*? I hardly think God was trying to communicate a fairness message. I don't think God was particularly interested in humanity's interpretation of fairness. Since God is spiritual, what was He possibly communicating in the spiritual realm? While there are many lessons we can learn from this parable, I don't think we can miss His message concerning the sovereignty of God. Yes, God is sovereign! That's clear from the Matthew passage. And humankind will probably always be unhappy with God's decision as to what *He* determines is *fair*. God's sovereignty isn't all about us! It doesn't necessarily align with what humanity wants.

WHEN IT DOESN'T GO OUR WAY...

When God doesn't perform as we've decided He should, when we don't receive the fairness we feel we deserve—when we don't receive those tangible outcomes—we panic and have to conclude that either *God is not good* or *we have failed* somehow in our life, making it necessary for a fair God to punish us or deny us what we deserve! Either of these options can be used to explain the *unfairness* that causes disappointment, depression, or even anger to set in. Once again, when truth surfaces, as it must, it will inevitably cause all kinds of conflicts and struggles in the mind. The *truth* is that God doesn't see fairness as humankind sees fairness; therefore, God will never respond as humanity would like Him to respond.

The reason, however, that this idea of fairness causes such anger, disappointment, and angst is that whether we're a vineyard worker from Matthew 20, a client who wanted a cookie-baking mom, or a wall street broker, when *we* determine the standard for fairness, we will always be let down. We will determine our perfect ten, but we are always changing—our desires, our emotions, our goals, our maturity, etc. Therefore, our perfect ten is also always changing, making it more and more impossible to ever attain—hence disappointment. Only when we adhere to God's understanding of fairness can we ever hope to be at peace, because God's standard never changes.

GOD'S VIEW OF FAIRNESS

So let's look at how God views fairness. As I study this passage and several others in the Scriptures, I frankly see no indication that God values humanity's interpretation of fairness at all. Some might look at the principles of sowing and reaping as a clue to God's fairness, but these are general principles based on logic. If I eat 5,000 calories each day, I will probably gain weight. We reap what we sow. If I work harder and longer hours than the guy in the cubicle next to me, I will probably get promoted before him. We reap what we sow. They are not principles based on entitlement or works. In Jesus' day, He abhorred the popular thought that so many shared of earning your way to Heaven to salvation.

And notice, fairness is not listed as one of God's attributes or His characteristics. Nor is fairness listed as one of the fruits of the Spirit, the characteristics that God values and therefore wants us to manifest, which are listed in Galatians 5:22—love, joy, peace, patience, kindness, goodness, faithfulness, gentleness, and self-control.

The truth is that I don't believe God is fair! Why? Because fair is merely a human term born out of sin and pride. We've shown many of the problems with this term *fair*. I believe God chose "unfair" principles for this world so that He might display His greater attributes of righteousness, mercy, and grace.

GOD'S GREATER BLEND OF RIGHTEOUSNESS, MERCY, AND GRACE

Righteousness is defined as "acting in a just upright manner, doing what is right." People love that definition as long as it is right for them! We know that God is righteous. Only He is always doing what is right. Only He is perfect. Only God can truly be righteous and not sin.

For the Lord is righteous, He loves justice (Psalm 11:7)

Righteous are You, O Lord, and Your laws are right (Psalm 119:137).

The Lord is righteous in all His ways and loving toward all He has made (Psalm 145:17).

Now there is in store for me the crown of righteousness, which the Lord, the righteous Judge, will award to me on that day (2 Timothy 4:8).

We also know that God is merciful. *Mercy* is defined as "refraining from harming or punishing offenders, enemies."[3] The Christian community often refers to mercy as withholding from us what we deserve. Well, that certainly doesn't satisfy my need for fair—*unless* I happen to be on the receiving end of mercy.

I will have mercy on whom I will have mercy, and I will have compassion on whom I will have compassion (Exodus 33:19).

Therefore God has mercy on whom He wants to have mercy, and He hardens whom He wants to harden (Romans 9:18).

Because judgment without mercy will be shown to anyone who has not been merciful. Mercy triumphs over judgment (James 2:13).

Grace is defined as "the unmerited love and favor of God toward humankind."[4] The Christian community often refers to grace as giving us what we *don't* deserve. Wow, that sounds *unfair*! But if it were not for God's grace, none of us could ever be saved.

Now Stephen, a man full of God's grace and power, did great wonders and miraculous signs among the people (Acts 6:8).

…The grace of our Lord Jesus be with you (Romans 16:20).

For it is by grace you have been saved, through faith— and this not from yourselves, it is the gift of God—not by works, so that no one can boast (Ephesians 2:8-9).

If God had chosen *fairness* to be displayed on this earth, He certainly wouldn't have sent His *perfect, sinless Son* to leave His magnificent throne in Heaven and come to this dirty earth to be beaten and bludgeoned for the sake of us sinners! What's *fair* about that? Nothing! If God had really chosen fair, we would all be on our way to *hell* for eternity. If God acted only out of His *righteousness*, He would have only done what was *right*, and we would all be doomed for hell.

Instead, God chose to perfectly *blend* His righteousness (it is right that sin must be paid for) with His attribute of mercy (God withholding what we all really deserve, hell, because Romans 3:23 states, *"All have sinned and fall short of the glory of God"*), with His grace. (Ephesians 2:8-9 states, *"For it is by grace you have been saved, through faith—and this not from yourselves, it is the gift of God—not by works, so that no one can boast."* He gives us all eternity in Heaven with our Lord, which we absolutely don't deserve.) Nothing about this scenario is *fair* based upon humanity's definition of fair. Fair is too self-centered a concept for God to own. Thank God for that fact, or we would all be doomed.

SO YOU WANT FAIR?

We foolishly cry out for fair but never sit back and really contemplate the consequences of a world that was truly fair. Truly *fair* would result in me getting a speeding ticket every time I drove on I-95, as I rarely go the exact speed limit. (Mercy.)

Truly *fair*? For generations women were such second-class citizens that I couldn't possibly have had an excellent education and career, but *unfair* had me born at a time that I could spread my wings with all kinds of exciting choices in life. (Grace.)

Truly fair might have me born in an African village where AIDS is so rampant that it would be just a matter of time before I would have it and would orphan my children. Or possibly have me born in a country where burkas are the fashion and the name of Christ can only be spoken in a whisper. (Mercy.)

Truly *fair*? When our house was blown up several years ago during a hurricane, only because we "fortunately" live in the United States and therefore can buy insurance, could we not lose our home. If I really wanted fair, do you realize that every time I eat in a restaurant where numerous people are handling my food, many of whom could be sick, I have a "fair" chance of getting sick. Instead, I am happily full, and happy that I didn't have to cook or do the dishes. (Grace.)

Every time people answer their cell phones or begin texting someone while driving, *fair* would probably result in a car accident. Every day God chooses *humankind's unfairness* and instead demonstrates His perfectly balanced righteousness, mercy, and grace.

BACK TO PHILIPPIANS 4:8

So what do we do when clients come into the office, feeling depressed because they feel somehow God hasn't been *fair* to them? The truth is that I can't mend the broken heart of a sweet, young woman who was sitting, seatbelt on, at a red light, only to be plowed into by a woman going 50 miles per hour who was talking on her cell phone. After one year of hospitalization and rehab, this young woman will never fully recover her eyesight, limiting her job opportunities substantially for the rest of her life. And to make matters worse, the driver was without insurance and only owned her 10-year-old car. *Unfair?* Absolutely.

When a little girl comes in who has been sexually abused by her granddaddy? Heartbreaking and unfair? Absolutely.

When parents come in having lost their only child to a drunk driver? Crushing and unfair? Absolutely.

When people come into the office feeling depressed or disappointed over what they perceive to be God's or life's unfairness, where do we go? We begin with God's direction of course. Philippians 4:8 instructs us first to meditate on *truth*. We acknowledge the person's loss that seemed unfair to them in the *physical realm*.

Rejoice with those who rejoice; mourn with those who mourn (Romans 12:15).

We later move on to acknowledge God's truth is the spiritual realm. We meditate on what is true, noble, right, pure, lovely, admirable, excellent, and praiseworthy. In other words, we begin to praise God for choosing the *unfair* in this world. I know that had God not allowed *unfair* principles to be part of our lives on this planet, not only would all life as we know it be far worse for all of us, but we would all be spending eternity in hell. Life goes so quickly that it is described as only a vapor in the Book of James. But eternity? *Forever* is something the human mind can't even conceive. That's meditating on truth—God's truth, not man's truth. We meditate on God's excellent plan for life and salvation combined with a plan to display *His* glory, *His* righteousness, *His* mercy, and *His* grace. He alone is worthy of praise.

QUESTIONS

1) List ways that people want "fair" in their lives.

2) Would you be willing to share which of these you might have struggled with?

3) What do you believe is the reason, both righteous and sinful, that people want fairness so badly?

4) Describe some of the consequences in our lives if we really got what we asked for—fairness!

5) What are some of the behaviors you exhibit when you don't get what you believe is fair?

6) List as many messages as you can speak to yourself to pull out of the "pity party" of unfairness. Remember, they all must be truthful.

Chapter 5

THE TRUTH ABOUT
ANXIETY, PANIC ATTACKS, AND AGORAPHOBIA

Wow, what a marvelous mechanism from God!

THREE NEW CLIENTS

Several weeks ago, I took on three new clients in my practice, each manifesting the same problems. All three of these clients had gone to the hospital emergency room with symptoms that mimicked a possible heart attack. All three of these clients were put through a battery of tests before being released and told they were fine, that they were having panic attacks. One of the clients ended up at the emergency room a total of three times before she finally resigned herself to the fact that she wasn't dying of a heart attack.

Panic attacks are described as:

> Periodic, discrete bouts of panic that occur abruptly and reach a peak within 10 minutes. Such attacks consist of

at least four symptoms of panic, the most common of which are heart palpitations, tingling in the hands or feet, shortness of breath, sweating, hot and cold flashes, trembling, chest pains, choking sensations, faintness, dizziness, and a feeling of unreality.[1]

People often complain that these attacks came out *of the blue* or when they were simply at home alone totally not expecting them, as they were not stressed in any way.

Many people are given prescriptions for drugs such as Zanax, which is designed to calm individuals down so they can function in their everyday jobs, sleep at night, etc. We have several *possible* problems, however, with these drugs. Note I said *possible*. Drugs such as Zanax can be highly addictive and are often seen as an end to the problem rather than as a bridge or a tool to take us from illness to wellness. However, they can be an extremely useful tool when used properly. Drugs are given to us by God to help us in difficult times. What would we do without the opiates that keep us pain free after surgery or during a prolonged illness? God gave us these drugs for good purposes. It's man and woman who often distort their usefulness.

ANXIETY AND PANIC ATTACKS DEFINED

So what are these anxiety or panic attacks we're hearing about so often during these historically stressful times? Mr. Webster defines *anxiety* as "a state of being uneasy, apprehensive, or worried about what may happen; concern about a possible future event."[2] *Panic* is defined as "a sudden, unreasoning hysterical fear, often spreading quickly."[3]

Now let's look at these two definitions and size up how they are different and yet connected. To begin with, we must realize that were it not for anxiety, humankind would probably not be able to survive! If I didn't have a "state of being uneasy, apprehensive, or worried about what may happen; concern about a possible event," I would not think twice about letting my 2-year-old granddaughter roam around outside by herself near the pool or the roadway. Were it not for the anxiety mechanism in my body, I would never think about crossing a main road without looking to the right or the left. Were it not for anxiety, I would never have doctor visits to check my cholesterol levels, nor would I ever get a mammogram.

God *wonderfully* placed this anxiety system in our bodies for our *protection*. He did not create this species called humankind without giving us built-in protections for our survival. It is appropriate that we have "concern about a possible future event." Isn't that the basis for the government setting up Medicare programs so that we have medical care when we are no longer working for a company that provides healthcare insurance? Isn't that the reason for our Social Security programs, our 401Ks, and our Roth IRAs, so that we are financially protected in the future long after retirement? Isn't that why I don't have a hot fudge sundae every night but space them out so I don't end up with diabetes like my mother and grandmother? (That last question might better be explained by admitting it is my vanity that keeps me in check concerning weight, since this is a book about *truth*!)

The *truth* is that we would not be able to survive as a species if it were not for that *anxiety mechanism*. Now, before I continue, I must address what I know many readers are thinking about. (Remember, I'm a psychotherapist.) Philippians 4:6-7 states:

> *Do not be anxious about anything, but in everything, by prayer and petition, with thanksgiving, present your requests to God. And the peace of God, which transcends all understanding, will guard your hearts and your minds in Christ Jesus.*

MUDDLED CHRISTIAN MENTALITY

If I could count the number of Christians who believe this verse should be interpreted to mean that they must just "give everything to God, not think about the problem again, let it all go, and God will handle it all," I would have to empty out half of my Christian client files. This kind of thinking is not from God. This is a muddled distortion of the *truth* of God's Word, or more simply, put this is La-La Land! This kind of thinking is often employed by Christians who are in denial about the reality of problems in life and sadly choose these beliefs, as it gives the appearance of being a more *lofty* or *spiritual* Christian who is above such concern or worry. This thinking is also chosen by the Christian who just doesn't want to seek a deeper understanding of an event or who simply doesn't want to do the work of changing. I believe we can safely label this kind of unrealistic thinking *Christianese Psychobabble!*

The Greek word *anxious* does not mean we shouldn't think or meditate about a problem. Nor does it mean that we should not roll up our sleeves and deal with a problem. It does mean we are not to *dwell* on a problem.

God gave us the cortex portion of the brain that we are to use to think and meditate. The cortex is used to employ logic, deal with issues, make adjustments based on wisdom and intelligence, alter strategies, and essentially problem solve! No other creature was given this portion of the brain. Why? Because we all know difficulties will befall us. Jesus said it in John 16:33, *"In this world you will have trouble."* I believe it; we've all experienced it.

GOD'S WARNING SYSTEM—ANXIETY

The truth is that God gave us all a warning system, *anxiety*, to help us concerning difficult or dangerous future events, and then gave *only humans* a brain to deal with these problems so that we can have that "life and life abundant" He wants for us. When we choose to buy into the unrealistic expectation, the lie, telling ourselves not to think about the difficulty and just "give it all to God," then we don't have to employ that part of the brain to deal with anxious or difficult possible future situations. When we simply choose to buy the *unrealistic lie*, we might as well accept that we are as *unintelligent* as every four-legged creature that roams the earth and wasn't blessed with that magnificent and complex cortex for problem solving.

This kind of thinking, believing the lie, sets us up for an incredible amount of disappointment and depression every time we choose to *do nothing, but expect* God to do everything. The result will often be the absence of well resolutions, changed directions, and changed lives. We end up *disappointed* with God for not doing what He *never* told us He would do. Instead, He gave us wonderful tools to get the job done! If we unrealistically believe that all choices are *out* of our hands, we deny God's incredible handiwork in the creation of the human brain and body. We also deny His plan to give each one of us a *free will* to exercise various choices.

PANIC DEFINED

That brings us to our next definition regarding the word *panic*. Unlike the definition for anxiety, panic is defined as a "sudden unreasoning hysterical fear." This is very different from our more thoughtful anxiety definition, which demonstrates "worry over what might happen; concern about a possible future event." The word *hysterical* is defined as "emotionally uncontrolled and wild,"[4] which would make *panic* a *product* of "unreasoning and emotionally uncontrolled and wild fears." And this would be a pretty accurate description of panic attacks suffered by so many. Why? Because a panic attack is rarely reasonable after it has been broken down and dissected. Nothing about it is orderly or peaceful. Hmm! That certainly reminds me of a verse: *"For God is not the author of confusion, but of peace, as in all churches of the saints"* (1 Cor. 14:33 NKJV).

Would it be safe to say that if the description of panic is contrary to what God states that He is the author of, could it be that this confusion, hysteria, and chaos is from satan himself to "seek, kill, and destroy" (see John 10:10) our peace, joy, and lives? How logical.

Whereas anxiety is geared to protect one's life or future, to stir us to use the gifts and tools given to each one of us by God for wellness, panic is a counterfeit fear designed to create hysteria and confusion. It is designed to rob us of our joy and safety, as it doesn't result in resolution of a problem but in the escalation of a problem.

ANXIETY AND PANIC

Let's investigate this further. While sleeping, if people are awakened by sounds outside, anxiety might begin to well up inside them. They might wonder if someone is at the house—possibly trying to enter the house. Or could it just be an animal, possibly a raccoon near the garbage cans? That anxiety might prompt a person to get out of bed and look out of a window to seek some answers. My sister experienced that exact event years ago to find an intruder entering her porch. Upon seeing her, he ran off, thank goodness. The feelings of anxiety might prompt people to call 911, make sure the doors were all securely locked, and be generally vigilant until they believe the danger has passed. This anxiety, concern for a possible future event, might save a person's life and the life of his or her family.

If, on the other hand, people lay in bed night after night listening for every little sound, "unreasonably, emotionally and hysterically fearful" of what might occur, they have allowed panic to piggyback that excellent, God-given anxiety response given to us for the purpose of safety. The result is that one will be robbed of sleep, peace, health, and joy.

FIGHT AND FLIGHT

This immediate short-term anxiety is called the *fight–flight* response as the brain communicates to the body that it must prepare to either *fight* the possible intruder or *flee* the scene. Either way, this response is designed to protect the organism. I believe it's one of the most exciting mechanisms known to man and given to us by God! I will attempt to describe it.

When the brain contemplated the possibility of an intruder in our earlier example, it became anxious and went into action by beginning to communicate to the body that it must prepare to protect itself by either gearing itself up and fighting, or by preparing to flee the scene, also a choice to protect itself. When the body becomes anxious, it triggers the body's *sympathetic nervous system*, which releases the chemicals of adrenalin and cortisol. When the sympathetic nervous system is in control of the body, there is an increase in the heart rate and the strength of the heartbeat, which helps to speed up the blood flow. Blood is suddenly redirected to the places it is most needed like the quadriceps, the large muscles in the legs, in order to give the person added speed in the event a person must run or take action. *Magnificent!*

As blood decreases in the extremities because it is on its way to the more vital organs (the heart and lungs must be protected), there is often a tingling or numbness in the extremities, namely the arms, fingers, feet, and toes, etc. Many people feel that tingling or numbness and believe it's the early signs of a stroke or a heart attack. The truth is that if the intruder attacks the person, shoots or knifes them in the leg, for example, they are far less apt to bleed to death when there is less blood in these extremities. *Marvelous!*

There are additional changes that occur in the body to protect the organism. When the flight-fight system is activated, an increased sweating occurs. This serves two purposes. For one thing, the body will be more slippery, making it more difficult for the intruder to grab or catch the person. Furthermore, it acts to cool the body down, making it less apt to overheat, which is pretty common during times of stress. *Brilliant!* But how often does a person misinterpret that sweating as a symptom of severe illness?

THE SYMPATHETIC NERVOUS SYSTEM

When the fight-flight response and the sympathetic nervous system are activated, changes also occur in the person's breathing, once again for the purpose of protecting the organism. There is an increase in the speed and depth of breathing. This is for the purpose of getting more oxygen to the tissues to better prepare the body for the action it needs to take for protection. This deeper, faster breathing actually causes the blood supply to the head to decrease, especially if no actual activity occurs. Once again, if "blunt force trauma" occurs to the head, an expression regularly heard on every cop show on TV, the person is far less apt to bleed to death from a head injury because there is simply less blood in the brain area. *Fantastic!*

A well-known actress named Natalie Richardson died in March 2009 when she had a simple fall on a bunny slope while skiing in Canada with her family. She got right up after the fall and turned away the paramedics, stating she felt fine. Only several hours later, she was unconscious because that simple fall had damaged an artery in her brain, causing internal bleeding, which resulted in an "epidural hematoma due to blunt impact to the head."[5] The collection of blood pressed the brain down, causing brain death. All of this occurred within hours of a simple fall. Her fans and family were shocked at such a sudden, unexpected turn of events. She was soon taken off of life support and died. The simple decrease of blood to the head, which occurs during times of stress could prove vital to saving a person's life.

THE BODY'S SIDE EFFECTS

There are some side effects, however, when the body goes into a "deeper and increased breathing and a decreased blood flow to the head." That increased breathing can cause breathlessness, choking, or smothering feelings, as well as pains or a tightness in the chest. And the decreased blood flow in the head can cause symptoms of dizziness, blurred vision, confusion, unreality, and even hot flashes. Aren't these symptoms that again mimic the symptoms of a heart attack or stroke? So this magnificent fight-flight system given to us for our protection, *if perceived incorrectly* (Do I hear the beginning of yet another lie?) could be mistakenly interpreted as a life-threatening illness.

VISION

Vision is also affected when the body goes into fight-flight mode. The pupils become more dilated to allow as much light in as possible. Again, this is for the purpose of better vision to protect the species, especially to help if night vision is required. *Amazing!* The problem that occurs when the pupils widen, however, is that it can result in blurred vision or spots in front of the eyes, which often causes a person to be fearful that something is seriously wrong with him or her.

DIGESTIVE SYSTEM

There is also a decrease in the efficiency of the digestion system as the blood has moved from this location to the more vital areas of the body. Have you ever noticed that when stressed, you tend to lose your appetite? You're just not hungry! Digestion isn't working as usual, which can not only lessen the appetite but can also cause nausea, a heavy feeling in the stomach, dry mouth, and even constipation. These are symptoms I hear about all the time in my office from clients who are suffering from prolonged anxiety or panic attacks.

People are constantly worried because they've lost their appetite or are suffering from these other symptoms believing that something might be wrong with them physically, when the truth is that an *awesome Designer* created a body to automatically give itself the best shot at self-protection.

ACHES AND PAINS

Aches and pains? These are also a by-product of that fight-flight response system as the body's muscles tend to tense up during stress for the purpose of quick preparation for attack or escape. Unfortunately, the resulting symptoms of muscle tension manifest in more frequent headaches, muscle aches due to the tension, as well as trembling and shaking also due to tightened muscles.

OXYGEN INTAKE

I challenge my readers to close your eyes for just a moment and envision a truck is about to run you over on the road. What does your body suddenly do as you see that truck about to hit you? You gasp, of course, which is actually the body's way of attempting to save your life by sucking in life-protecting oxygen with the hope of giving you your best chance of survival until the paramedics arrive. *Stunning!*

Have you ever observed a moment when a man, in particular, puffs up his chest when he's about to deal with a difficulty, confront an issue, or enter a courtroom or a problematic meeting? Who would ever for a moment contemplate the fact that it is the body's *automatic* or *involuntary* actions that cause the person to puff up the chest, as it is for the purpose of filling the lungs up with life-giving oxygen in the event of attack/fight or flight. Such an action is, of course, under the radar of the conscious brain. No man or woman considers the logic of sucking in oxygen prior to a difficulty in the event an "attack" could occur.

AN AWESOME DESIGNER

It's stunning to observe so many unrealized physical occurrences designed, and I believe the operative word is *designed* to guide and protect this species called humankind. These body changes are too amazing to think for a moment they were "happenstance" but rather designed by a most-*awesome* Designer.

CREATED FOR A WORLD THAT
NO LONGER EXISTS

As you will read in our last chapter on the sympathetic/parasympathetic nervous systems, we will point out that the body was made for a world that no longer exists. The body was designed to adjust to those occasional *real* threats such as a tiger near your local cave home or in today's world, an intruder trying to enter your home for evil purposes. But at what point do we shift from God's healthy anxiety given to us for protection to those *panic attacks* that are so prevalent in our society today?

The best way to understand this is to contemplate the fact that anxiety was created to protect us from *physical death*. But in this extremely stressful twenty-first, death and dying have taken on an entirely new meaning. While anxiety is still for the purpose of protecting us physically, humankind now views death and dying in numerous complicated ways. Daily, many people fear death and dying of *marriages* as we watch the divorce rate nationally climb to approximately 50 percent for first marriages, 67 percent for second marriages, and 74 percent of third marriages.[6] We fear death and dying of *financial security,* which has people restlessly up all night. We fear death and dying of friendships, engagements, of neighbor friends and church families as people move. We fear death and dying of jobs, of our youth and looks, etc.

Anxiety is defined as "uneasiness, concern over a possible future event." But humanity has transferred that concern or anxiety to *perceived threats* rather than *real physical threats*. These threats will not end our lives physically, but the brain isn't differentiating between *perceived* or *real*. It's only hearing threats. This is a new level of anxiety due to the complicated world we live in, which has now birthed *chronic* or continual anxiety and stress.

SOME EXAMPLES OF CONTINUAL ANXIOUS AND STRESSFUL THOUGHTS

I'm worried about getting to work on time.

I'm worried about whether I turned off the coffee maker on my way out the door. I don't want a fire!

I'm worried I don't have enough money in the checking account to cover the mortgage payment.

I'm worried that none of the guys at the book study will even notice I'm there, and it's my first time.

I'm worried something is really wrong with me. I'm afraid if I go to the doctor, he might find something wrong. Maybe I'll just wait to see if the symptoms go away.

I'm worried I won't have a date to the prom. I'm the only one in our group who hasn't been asked yet.

I'm worried I'm running low on gas. I'll just cross my fingers I get to work okay and will get to a gas station as soon as I get out of work.

I'm worried that I have a ton of e-mails to check when I get home since I haven't checked my e-mail for several days. The thought of a new 100 to look at makes me feel overwhelmed.

The problem with this kind of thinking is that *chronic* concern or anxiety is exactly contrary to God's instruction of what to meditate on according to Philippians 4:8 and First Thessalonians 5:16. Hmmm. Now, I wonder if a sovereign God who is omnipresent was looking far beyond early man who lived with tigers in his backyard when He instructed us as to how to think? I wonder who might have the better plan for our lives to give us that life abundant that we all would like to have, God or humanity? Doesn't the watchmaker know best how to fix the watch? Doesn't the Creator of humankind know best how to fix broken and stressed lives?

WHEN CHRONIC STRESS BECOMES OUR NORMAL

Furthermore, *chronic* stress can eventually become our *normal*, and whatever our *normal* is, we will re-create again and again as automatically as breathing. Whatever our *normal* becomes will be followed with what we call *automatic thoughts,* which are thoughts that "arise as if they were a reflex, without prior reflection or reasoning."[7] The more often we stress, the more normal it becomes, and the more normal it becomes, the more we *automatically* think stressfully to the point that stress actually controls us rather than us controlling it.

I love to liken this principle of *automatic thoughts* to our new high-tech cell phones. When I begin to type a number into my cell phone that I call often, I rarely only get to three out of the ten digits, and my very smart cell phone automatically produces the number I was going to call faster than I was even able to type it in! This is the way the brain works. Thoughts or beliefs that are already there (chronic ways of thinking) shoot up into the brain faster than I can even conjure them up by themselves. If stressful thinking has become a regular or normal way of thinking, then it shoots up to the forefront of the brain even before we think about the fact that something might or might not be stressful. The *body* then begins to react automatically to the brain's *stress cry* and then begins disseminating the various body symptoms given to the body to protect us. *This is why people suddenly had a panic attack when they were not even consciously thinking about anything stressful!*

All anxiety is initiated by the "fear of death and dying" in order to protect the species. When the brain communicates danger to the body, the body automatically responds to the protection call and begins to manifest all those bells and whistles for fight or flight that we've described. But remember, the brain doesn't differentiate between *real* or *perceived danger, real* or *perceived fears.* The body will simply take its cue—*fear*—and begin the process regardless of the *reality.*

MY HOME-GROWN DEFINITION OF PANIC

Panic, therefore, is nothing more than anxiety combined with gobs of humankind's "unreasonable perceived, not realistic, fears over death and dying of some kind," mixed together with a pinch of "sudden attack" and stirred together to create a bowl full of "hysterical fear." That new creation is then piggybacked onto some unsuspecting person who has already made worry and anxiety their "chronic job." Suddenly, they're experiencing a full-blown panic attack because those protective body changes have just been transferred to a perceived threat that has become so automatic in their thought patterns that they don't even see it coming!

LAINEY AND KEN

Let me give an example of how this whole thing snowballs. I had a lovely young couple come into my office last year. They had a beautiful baby girl who was only several weeks old. This couple couldn't have been more delighted with the birth of their little one. But unfortunately, the mother had been experiencing panic attacks that had become so severe that they were seriously interfering with her daily functioning with her newborn.

After further investigation, I found out that this couple had been trying to conceive a child for years. They were in great pain with every mention of a baby shower or the pregnancy of a friend or neighbor. They went through years of anguish, medical testing, body probing, shots, and pills—all those dreadful procedures one must endure when faced with infertility and the desperate desire to have that little one in their arms. Finally, they went through the expense and stress of artificial insemination. On the day this young woman was going to be inseminated, members of her family spent the day praying and fasting. Oh, the joy! Lainey actually became pregnant! Everyone in the family couldn't have been happier for this godly young couple, and needless to say, they were ecstatic!

Then the day of delivery came. Yes, there were some complications, but mother and baby ended up just fine. But after the delivery, Ken would describe the birth experience and comment on the fact that he watched as his little baby girl actually turned blue. He remembers describing to hospital visitors the fear he felt as he recalled all that they had gone through to birth this little one. Then within days of going home with their baby, Mom began to become breathless, lightheaded, and shaking. Full-blown panic attacks! Why? Her dreams had finally come true! Shouldn't she have been on top of the world? God had answered their prayers and even protected both Mom and baby when danger presented itself in the delivery room. This made no sense to the couple, but she was almost becoming worse with each passing day.

WHAT TOOK PLACE IN THE BRAIN

Here's what happened in the brain. Lainey and Ken went through years of anxiety and stress trying to conceive. The brain began to experience "death and dying" of the dream of becoming parents, death and dying of going to little league games, of homeschooling, of days at the beach watching their babies eat the sand and collect shells, of going with their friends to the Mommy and Me classes, and of the experience of seeing "his eyes" and "her sandy hair." Couples who have been trying for some time to conceive often report a constant scanning of the landscape for children, mothers with strollers, daddies at McDonald's, etc. Clients have shared with me their draw to follow mothers with babies in their shopping carriages at the grocery store, only to fill up with tears after watching mother and baby interact. Sadly, each observation often causes them to subliminally relive the *death and dying of a dream.*

Then the miracle of birth occurred for this couple! But suddenly, anxiety was introduced when the fear of death and dying became a *real threat*, an actual possible death and dying of their child in the delivery room. The child they had so longed for, prayed for, and waited for turned blue before their very eyes. At this point, Lainey's brain began to communicate anxiety to the body, "a state of being uneasy, apprehensive, worried about what may happen; concern about a possible future event," and she began to manifest all those built-in body changes designed to protect the body (i.e., breathing changes, adrenalin levels elevated, sweating, etc.).

Now we move on to *panic attacks* when we combine gobs of humans' "unreasonable perceived fears over death and dying" (unreasonable because the baby was alive and well) with years of *chronic anxiety* due to fear of death and dying memories of perhaps never having a child, mixed with a pinch of *sudden attack* (the moment that she heard her husband describe her baby's color probably kept spinning around in her subliminal brain), stirred all together to create a bowl of *hysterical fear* (hysterical is defined as emotionally uncontrollable and wild—the frantic experience of panic attacks!).

This new creation was now *piggybacked* onto a person who already had years of anxiety over the desperate desire to experience the *life* of her dream of a child, but instead she had to face the fear of a possible *real death.* The protective body changes that surfaced in Lainey when the brain read *danger,* while they were now only perceived threats (perceived because the child was alive and healthy), were, nonetheless, still read in the brain as *threatening danger.*

They never saw it coming. It made no sense to a couple who was happier than any other time in their lives! But once we begin to understand this marvelous mechanism given to us by God to protect us, we can follow the logical progression of a *truth* with a hint of a *lie* thrown in. The lie in this case was that she or her baby had anything to fear. Both were alive and well. The lie was that the "death and dying" were read in the body as *real* rather than *perceived.*

WHY THEN CAN'T PEOPLE JUST GET OVER IT ONCE THEY REALIZE THE TRUTH?

You see, once the brain is signaled that a danger is present, it *must* go into protection mode, and once the body changes have begun, the brain *must* scan and search for the real danger. When it realizes there is nothing to actually be fearful of (i.e., both Mom and baby are in perfect health), the *brain will eventually turn inward* and *grasp one* of those *physical changes*, perhaps the rapid heartbeat and lightheadedness, as a real physical threat or danger to justify its response.

Why did this young woman experience more severe panic attacks each day? Because when the brain realized there was nothing to fear, Mom and baby were safe, the brain turned inward, became fearful of some of those physical changes that could easily mimic heart attack symptoms, and communicated danger to the organism, the mom, to justify its response. Mom's brain, *now fearful of the body changes,* perceived danger and must manifest more body changes to prepare for fight or flight, which caused her more fear, which caused more body changes, and *on and on* the cycle went, getting worse each day! This is why a person just can't get over the attacks once he or she realizes the truth. *The entire process begins to take on a life of its own.*

JUST WATCHING TV

For example, a person watching TV might view a scene at a place of employment and suddenly wonders if he might be in the next group of job layoffs at his place of employment. The fleeting thought of fear crosses his mind. The loss of a job, a possible future concern enters the brain as the fear of death and dying of financial security, and he suddenly begins to experience the physical body changes commonly associated with anxiety and fight-flight, shortness of breath, tingling in the arms, etc. Suddenly he states, "I must be having a heart attack, or why else would I have all this tingling in my arm?" or "I feel so spacey and lightheaded; I think I'm having a stroke." *Now* the body has a legitimate cause for concern, and the fight-flight mechanism can continue.

THE MORE FEARFUL PEOPLE ARE OVER THEIR SYMPTOMS, THE MORE SYMPTOMS THEY WILL HAVE

At this point, people end up in the emergency room for real fear of "death or dying" as they *are* experiencing true symptoms. The more fearful and panic-stricken people are over physical symptoms, the more symptoms they will inevitably produce. The more symptoms they produce, the more fear they experience. The more fear, the more symptoms. And on and on the cycle goes. The brain then logs the entire incident into its memory bank, making the cycle pop up much faster the next time perceived threats begin the body's automatic responses, and pretty soon a person's perceived threats regularly become true threats and fears over physical symptoms that cause a person to really be fearful. Hence, panic sets in! Wow, do I see the author of confusion in this scenario? And isn't satan also the father of lies? Once again, what God gave man and woman for good, the deceiver has turned to evil to rob our joy, peace, and very lives.

WILLIAM OUR BUSINESSMAN

Let's look at another example to give this crazy cycle some legs. A young man comes to the office, as he experienced panic attacks so bad that he must take a Zanax every time he presides over a sales meeting. Without the drugs, he can't breathe, feels faint and lightheaded, and is afraid he might pass out. Now, each time he even thinks of his sales meetings on Monday morning, he becomes panic-stricken and nauseous. He has no clue why this is happening. After some time together, I discovered he was divorced and painfully saddened because his ex-wife had engaged in parental alienation syndrome, or PAS, and now his little girl wanted nothing to do with him.

PAS is a systematic belittling of one parent by the other parent until a child hates, fears, and doesn't want anything to do with the belittled parent. This father couldn't see his daughter without her screaming for her mother, so he finally resigned himself to stop putting her through the weekly hysteria and let her stay with her mother, hoping that one day she would want to try and establish a relationship with him. He was grieving the *death* of one of the most precious relationships in his life. That fear and horror of death and dying sat continually in the recesses of his brain.

WILLIAM'S FIRST ATTACK

Then the first attack came on a Monday morning. As everyone gathered together for the Monday morning meeting, people began to chat about their weekend events with friends and family, but for him such talk only triggered thoughts of death and dying of the relationship he was grieving with his daughter. Then suddenly his body went into *protection mode*—heart beating stronger, deeper breathing, sweating, muscles tightening, arms tingling, etc. and he became so panic-stricken that he had to excuse himself, stating that he "simply didn't feel well." His brain read *fear* and *danger,* but as we have pointed out, the brain doesn't differentiate between *real physical* death and dying and *perceived* death and dying.

He later composed himself, hoping that dreadful episode would never happen again. But at the end of the week, he had to preside over another meeting. The brain, having recorded the earlier week's episode, subconsciously remembered all of the seemingly dangerous physical symptoms that William's body had gone through: heart palpitations, sweating, lightheadedness, nausea, etc. As William was preparing for his next meeting, quietly *fearful* and hoping that he wouldn't experience a similar physical episode to the one earlier in the week, William's brain heard his *fear* message, remembered all those dangerous physical symptoms, and signaled the body that it better go into *protection mode* once again. Now William's body began to experience all those terrible symptoms, not so much because of his daughter but due to the *physical* events of his last dreadful meeting. And so, his body, directed by the brain's recording of all the physical problems, began gearing up to protect him from what his body read as *danger.*

WHEN THE BRAIN TALKS
TO THE BODY

Brain to body—could William be having a heart attack or stroke? Could he pass out while presiding over the meeting? Could he throw up while presiding over the meeting? (That last thought alone would set a person up for fear!) *Brain to body, brain to body*—let's protect this guy called William!

William was now so fearful that he would lose control at the meeting, begin to sweat profusely, experience heart palpitations, etc., that he now *feared the symptoms*, which began the entire process of the body's protection mode to begin *all over again*. William now had *real* physical symptoms to become fearful of rather than *perceived symptoms*.

AGORAPHOBIA

Now, before we specifically address how to get out of these debilitating panic attacks, we need to take a look at *agoraphobia* and how it is a logical pattern of behavior if a person is experiencing panic attacks. Agoraphobia is defined as "an abnormal fear of being in open or public places."[8] People who suffer with agoraphobia often spend weeks in their homes, afraid to even go to the store for simple groceries.

I had a client years ago who was so agoraphobic that she would go into a panic attack at the very thought of taking the garbage to the end of the driveway. Another client had such severe panic attacks and agoraphobia that while trying to take a flight to Chicago, the pilot actually had to return to the gate so the client could get off the plane before takeoff, as the client was becoming completely hysterical, fearful he was having a heart attack and terribly scaring the other passengers. What a surprise that the client was flying to Chicago to attend a funeral.

Remember how our panic attack dad had to excuse himself from the sales meeting when he began to experience the attack? He began to manifest sweating, feelings of his heart beating more strongly, tingling in his arm, lightheadedness etc. Not only do those physical symptoms cause people to be afraid that there is something dreadfully wrong with their health, but on top of that fear, agoraphobic people begin to worry about losing control of their bodies in public!

THE AUTHOR'S FIRST PREGNANCY

When I was pregnant, I experienced six months of horrible nausea from sunrise to bedtime. I never left the house, except for doctor's visits, because I was so afraid I might throw up in public. I kept a pan in the car whenever I drove anywhere as a safety precaution as well as a stash of dry crackers in the car, which I continually shoved in my mouth. But as hard as I tried, I had several occasions of throwing up on a public street. How mortified I was. I remember wanting to wear a sign telling any passer-by that I was pregnant, not drunk. I was desperate each time to get back to my home where I was safe, where I could get sick all day long, and nobody was there so see me.

That's the principle of *agoraphobia*. People with panic attacks are so afraid of losing control of their bodies that fear begins to take over every time they even contemplate leaving their homes, where at least they are safe from humiliation or possible danger. Remember how our young dad began to feel the attack come on him every time he thought of leading a meeting? "What if I embarrass myself and faint, get nauseous, start shaking, or even have a heart attack, etc. If I passed out, could I fall and crack my skull? Could I lose my job when they see I'm incapable of even leading a simple meeting? Will my employees look at me differently?"

THE SAFETY OF HOME

Once people begin to experience the safety of home, they're so relieved that they're not suffering panic attacks in public that it reinforces—rewards, really—their choice to stay at home, which makes the thought of going out even more frightening. The more frightened people are at the prospect of going out and possibly losing control of their bodies in public, the more they will feel fear, the more they feel fear, the more they will feel the anxiety symptoms in their body, and the more they feel the anxiety symptoms, the more panic they experience when they go out in public, which confirms in their mind the need to remain at home—and the cycle goes on and on! Understanding how a person reaches the point of making panic attacks a part of life makes the choice of *agoraphobia* a logical one for both the brain and the body.

THE UNHEALTHY TRIFECTA

So what is the way to rid ourselves of this unhealthy trifecta of anxiety, panic attacks, and agoraphobia? This is always my favorite part of the therapy! The answer is *truth!* Speak the *truth!* Think the *truth!* Live the *truth!* Believe the *truth!* Know the *truth,* and the *truth* will set you free! And what is the truth in all of these instances? The *truth* is that *anxiety symptoms* were given to us by God and serve a marvelous purpose in the protection of the species called *man,* and what a fragile species we are. The truth is that it is the *lies about* this mechanism that distort the truth and create panic and agoraphobia, which rob us of full and abundant lives. The *truth* is that the person's body is not in danger of death and dying when he or she is suffering from panic attacks, regardless of how his or her body seems to be reacting.

Our young mom need not fear any longer. She and her baby are alive and well. When the symptoms begin to rise in her body, she needs to *praise* God for a mechanism created to protect her. She needs to tell herself the *truth* that she just needs to sort out the *real* from the *perceived threats* in this complicated brain of hers. In her case, she must acknowledge that her body is well but is merely reacting to the *fear of perceived loss* rather than *actual loss.* She needs to meditate on the *truth* and *joy* of God's amazing mechanism of anxiety, take a relaxing, deep breath, and praise God for answering this couple's many years of prayers for a baby of their own.

In the case of our panic-attack dad, he also needs to speak words of truth to himself again and again. He too needs to acknowledge that he is certainly not dying, but his mind and body are simply confusing feelings of fear over the death and dying of the lost relationship with his child with the fear of death and dying of the body due to so many physical symptoms that continue to frighten him. He too needs to praise God for *protective mode symptoms* that are given by God to protect his life and health, and then ask God to help him sort out the *truth* from the *lies* so he can move on to that life God wants for him—a life that can only be victorious when its foundation is truth. He needs to realize that this incredible mechanism of the brain has been infiltrated with lies. But that amazing brain given by a good God can also be used to try to problem solve a way to restore his relationship with his child one day in the future.

WHAT AN AMAZING MECHANISM

Do you realize that when we begin to praise God for this stupendous, absolutely psychedelic, and *breathtaking* anxiety mechanism that God has given to us to protect this fragile human race that He has created, we will begin to lessen and eventually eliminate our fear of anxiety symptoms, which will conversely end the panic attacks. When we begin to speak words to ourselves that are truthful, we will communicate joyful yet calming messages from the brain to the body, which will bring the body to a place of *restoration* and *relaxation*. Why? Because when we fill our thoughts with praise and truth rather than worry and fear, restorative systems take over the body and work to restore the organism to a healthy mental state.

When we meditate according to Philippians 4:8, we must begin with that which is first and foremost *truthful*:

> *Finally, brothers, whatever is true, whatever is noble, whatever is right, whatever is pure, whatever is lovely, whatever is admirable—if anything is excellent or praiseworthy—think about such things.*

Then we must give thanks in all circumstances.

Be joyful always; pray continually; give thanks in all circumstances, for this is God's will for you in Christ Jesus (1 Thessalonians 5:16-18).

When we use our brain and direct our thoughts according to His Word, the truth, we can't help but respond to His *genius anxiety mechanism*. We can't help but be awestruck by His greatness rather than our frailties. And oh, what a shock—we have such a fuller, more peaceful life.

QUESTIONS

1) Have you ever experienced any of the symptoms common to panic attacks i.e., heart palpitations, tingling in hands and feet, shortness of breath, sweating, giddiness, trembling, etc.? Do you believe you were experiencing a panic attack? Have you regularly suffered from panic attacks?

2) Describe how believing a "lie" or an "unrealistic expectation" could set us up for anxiety or fear.

3) Describe the difference in the word *anxiety* and *panic*. Explain why God actually gave us the mechanism of anxiety.

4) List some things that we would be wise to have anxiety over.

5) Many people move from anxiety over "real threats" to "perceived threats," which can lead to "chronic" anxiety and stress. What are some of the perceived threats that people are constantly worrying about which robs them of their peace?

Chapter 6

THE TRUTH ABOUT
THE SILENCE OF ADAM

LIFE IN PARADISE

L et's set the stage properly. In Genesis 3 we see the chapter labeled "The Fall of Man." Satan, also called the "father of lies," is gearing up for his memorable debut.

> *When he lies, he speaks his native language, for he is a liar and the father of lies* (John 8:44).

The setting is the Garden of Eden, *Eden* being a word synonymous with the word *Paradise*.[1] Genesis 2:8 informs us that God Himself planted the Garden. Can you imagine the beauty and diversity in a garden planted by the God of the entire universe? I often marvel at the numerous colors of flowers in my South Florida landscape—bright pinks, lavenders, golden yellows, etc. My eyes wander from palm trees to oak trees, from soaring pelicans over the water to little red cardinals that make their way to my bedroom window every spring, from lizards to ladybugs. But I suspect in God's personally planted garden there were colors that man has not yet dreamed of! It must have been nothing less than breathtaking.

ENTER OUR PLAYERS

Enter our first player, Adam, who was not only personally formed by God's own hands but who we're told received the breath of life by God when He breathed into Adam's nostrils.

> *The Lord God formed the man from the dust of the ground and breathed into his nostrils the breath of life, and the man became a living being* (Genesis 2:7).

Do you realize that Adam didn't inherit Uncle Harry's club feet or Grandpa Joe's premature receding hairline? There were no nasty old genetics to pass down. The first man handcrafted by God Himself. I can't help but imagine that the angels watched in awe.

And then we have beautiful Eve. I have to believe every one of her features were perfectly proportioned: young skin, no wrinkles, shining hair (no split ends from perms), clear eyes, and perfect white teeth (no coffee stains). This couple was lovingly formed and perfected by a Father who loved them so much that He would one day lay down His life for them.

Genesis 2:6 tells us that water bubbled up from the ground. Of course there were no chilling rains or breezes too cold because Adam and Eve were naked and apparently had no need for protective clothing in Paradise. This also eliminated weekend laundry duty. Neither of them were work weary at this point because there were no weeds, thorns, or thistles in the Garden yet to make Adam's work more difficult. And Eve had no exhausting, late-night baby feedings or teethings because they had no children. Nor did they have any in-laws or annoying neighbors dropping in unannounced, and the term "demanding bosses" was not even a word in their vocabulary. Suffice to say this *was* truly Paradise!

ADAM WAS NOT GOOD ALONE

Now it was clear to Adam that he was to lead this family of two. He was God's first human creation, and we learn in the second chapter of Genesis that as God created all of the beasts of the field and the birds of the air, they were brought to Adam so that he could name them. Genesis 2:20 states, *"But for Adam no suitable helper was found."* In Genesis 2:18, God states, *"It is not good for the man to be alone. I will make a helper suitable for him."* That "helper" was of course beautiful Eve.

What do we conclude from this? To begin with, Adam was obviously *not good alone*. I don't believe this was simply based on his inability to reproduce children. After this incredibly complex world and everything in it that God had just created, surely God could have handily created the mechanism to make it possible for Adam to have children had He chosen to.

However, if we look at the actuarial tables, we find that men are far less likely to remain single after the death of a spouse, as widowers remarry at a rate of 80 percent compared to the rate for widows, which is 25 percent.[2] Perhaps God saw a loneliness in Adam that couldn't be filled by God's spiritual presence alone. Perhaps Adam needed a physical touch. Perhaps he couldn't find his wallet or keys in the morning! We'll never fully have the question answered this side of Heaven, but we do know that Eve was made for a specific purpose: to come alongside and help Adam.

BE WHAT YOU WERE DESIGNED FOR

When I put on a dress specifically designed for my size, I feel very comfortable in it; I can work and play, do whatever my day calls for, and not fret or even think about the dress. But if someone hands me a size 4 and I try to wear it, I will be yanking it down, constantly adjusting it, and uncomfortably sucking in my stomach. I'll be miserable because it was not what I am specifically suited for. We are created to glorify a living God. Simply, put that means I want *His* marching orders done *His* way, and what a difference that makes in my daily walk. Only then am I wearing the dress I'm completely comfortable in, completely suited for. Only then am I walking freely, not worried about every step I'm taking. I am a married woman. I am one flesh with my husband; therefore, I am called by God to come alongside him to be a helpmate. Please note, however, that this in no way makes my husband more important to God than I am, nor does it make Adam more important than Eve. Both are equal in God's eyes.

> *There is neither Jew nor Greek, slave nor free, male nor female, for you are all one in Christ Jesus* (Galatians 3:28).

It simply gives her a different role. Absolute logic dictates that two captains on a ship will create mutiny. But both a captain and an engineer are necessary for smooth and safe sailing.

LET THE LIES BEGIN

In Genesis 2:16-17 Adam receives his first directive from God.

> *And the Lord God commanded the man, "You are free to eat from any tree in the garden; but you must not eat from the tree of the knowledge of good and evil, for when you eat of it you will surely die."*

While Eve was not yet created when this directive was given, it's clear that she was aware of this command given to her husband based on the conversation she had with the serpent in the first verses of Genesis 3. We also see the first hint at the Fall of Man the moment *the lies begin.* Life as Adam and Eve knew it would never be the same again, and so it is with every individual who enters my office. The *lies* that are whispered in our ears by the evil one or proclaimed loudly by a culture, church, or country that we love are the words that can begin our spiral downward.

The serpent asks Eve in Genesis 3:1, *"Did God **really** say, 'you must not eat from **any tree** in the garden?'"* (Lie #1.) God never said *"any tree."* Eve calls the serpent on the "any tree" comment, but then jumps into the deception with her own lie by stating:

> *We may eat fruit from the trees in the garden, but God did say, "You must not eat fruit from the tree that is in the middle of the garden, and **you must not touch it, or you will die**"* (Genesis 3:2-3).

This was lie #2. God never said they could not *touch the tree or they would die!* Well, now the serpent knows Eve's on board with him, and his next lie is a bold contradiction of God's truth. He states in Genesis 3:4, *"You will not surely die."*

THE LIES ARE THE SOURCE OF OUR PROBLEMS

Here we go, gang. The lies are creeping on in! It's *always* the source of our problems. Think for just a moment how every lie I tell myself or others serves to make me look more important in front of others, feel better about myself, and appear more righteous or deserving; essentially, my lies simply fuel my pride. What did satan's lie really communicate to Eve?

What a stingy God you serve, Eve.

You deserve so much more, Eve.

Imagine God not letting you eat from "any" tree in the Garden.

And what does Eve's lie back really communicate?

How mean a God who would make me die for just touching that tree.

The little lies begin to puff us up while bringing others down. This is 180 degrees opposite of how God calls us to live.

GOD'S HIGHER CALL

Do nothing out of selfish ambition or vain conceit, but in humility consider others more important than yourselves (Philippians 2:3).

As we look at satan's last bold lie where he states the woman would *not* surely die, we see satan is actually proclaiming superiority over God Himself—claiming authority over life, death, and God's proclamation. Talk about pride!

AGAPE LOVE—THE LOVE
WE LONG FOR

Enter the first heartbreak between a husband and wife. Genesis 3:6-7 states:

*When the woman saw that the fruit of the tree was good for food and pleasing to the eye, and also desirable for gaining wisdom, she took some and ate it. She also gave some to her husband, **who was there with her**, and he ate it. Then the eyes of both of them were opened, and they realized they were naked; so they sewed fig leaves together and made coverings for themselves.*

People the world over have swooned over the stories of Romeo and Juliet, Cinderella and Prince Charming, *Westside Story*, etc. Why?

Because they resonate in the hearts of each and every one of us in some way. It's what we all ache for—someone to love and respect us. Someone who will lift us above themselves. Someone who would lay down his or her life for us, who would slay the dragon for us!

That "love story" captures every heart, young and old. I recently put the Disney movie *Sleeping Beauty* on one afternoon while babysitting my 3-year-old granddaughter, Peyton. As she watched Princess Aurora and Prince Philip dancing to "I Knew You Once Upon a Dream," I saw her actually begin to move with the music, attempting to dance, completely captured in the mood of the *oneness*, while continuing to be fixated on this couple falling in love. She was experiencing more than a cartoon fairytale.

In the same way, a baby will scan the room searching for his mother, and only when he finds her does his little face radiate a joy and calm, knowing full well that he is both adored and protected. The realization that another would die for us takes us to the most secret core of our being, a place where our pride refuses to admit how desperate we really are for such a love as *agape love*, a completely self-sacrificial love.

WHERE'S THE DRAGON SLAYER?

Adam was called to lead and protect his bride. And what did he do as his beautiful love was about to embark on disaster? The woman that he had called "bone of my bones and flesh of my flesh," the woman he had become *one* with, the woman he had been completely vulnerable with—she was about to eat from a fruit that would bring about her death. There he sat, watching Eve take the first bite that would change the world—the first bite that God Himself stated would result in death (see Gen. 2:17).

He was there with her. Was Adam too gripped with fear to move? Was he thinking about running to stop Eve? Was he afraid to lead his wife? Was he curious about what death would look like? Was he sheepishly relieved that she was taking the first risk? Was he hoping that suddenly God would step in and stop Eve because he was afraid she would become angry at him if he tried to stop her? Did he tear up at the prospect of losing his love? Did he even care? Did he really love her after all? Adam was silent.

Now I do acknowledge that Adam might not have totally understood the meaning of death. Perhaps no animal had died as of yet. But he certainly understood it was *not good,* as God had stated it as a consequence of disobedience. Where is Eve's dragon slayer? Where is the one who would protect her with his very life? Where is the one whose own body she was created from, who called her "bone of my bones and flesh of my flesh"? Where was the one she had shared total intimacy with in one flesh, the metaphysical bonding of the sexual union?

GOD'S KEYS TO
A BEAUTIFUL MARRIAGE

I believe that God gave us the keys to a beautiful marriage in Ephesians 5:33 when he stated that *husbands must love* (agape) their wives as they love themselves and the *wife must respect* her husband. I believe what a woman longs for most, more than food or water, is *love.* Now ladies, I'm not referring to the feeling of love, and men I'm not referring to sex. I am referring to that Greek word God uses for love, *agape.* First John actually gives us a definition for this word.

> *This is how we know what love* [agape] *is: Jesus Christ laid His life down for us* (1 John 3:16).

This Greek word for love, *agapao,* was actually meant to replace man's selfish love with God's perfect sacrificial love. Man's love is based on the *object* of what they love, which is often based on the appealing qualities of that object. For example, I love her because "she is beautiful and fun to be with." "I love this person because he is exciting to be with." Or, "I love him because he is such a hard and successful worker."

The problem then becomes, what happens when she is no longer beautiful or has a grumpy day? What happens when he or she becomes infirm and is no longer exciting to be with? What happens when he loses his job and no longer appears successful? Human love is based on humanity's subjective feelings, and as long as that *other person* fits what appeals to me, I can continue to love him or her.

Agapao love was meant to replace humankind's subjective love, as it is defined as, "to esteem, to cherish, favor, be devoted...to prize, to treat as precious."[3] And better still, agapao love is rooted in the *mind* and therefore the *will of the person who loves* rather than the *object* to be loved; therefore, if the *object* changes, loses her beauty, or becomes less exciting or successful, it does not change the *fact* that he or she is still "esteemed, cherished, favored, prized, or treated as precious." To be loved regardless of my ugliness. Wow! God was calling us to love each other in a way we can barely comprehend, in a way God Himself loves.

> *My command is this: Love each other as I have loved you* (John 15:12).

ADAM WAS CALLED TO LEAD!

There He is, the true dragon slayer, the one who would die for us, Jesus Christ Himself. And why does God *first* command men to love their wives sacrificially in Ephesians 5:33? *Because Adam was supposed to be the leader,* of course. Adam was supposed to lead the family, to lead his wife. What woman doesn't thrill at such self-sacrificial leadership? It makes following a husband's leadership the simplest of tasks.

I have men constantly frustrated in my office by wives who try to lead or who battle their husband's leadership. Again and again I see the

Adam and Eve scenario played out. These men often angrily want their wives to go first in changing the family dynamics. They want their wives to *first* stop leading so they can lead the family, but that is doing nothing more than *reacting* to their wives, which is the exact opposite of what they need to do, which is to *lead* their wives with loving leadership.

To these men, I often want to scream, "Take the reins of leadership by loving your wife sacrificially, and she will yield herself to you!" But unfortunately, these men often communicate their frustration by withdrawing from their wives. When a man chooses to withdraw, he is actually relinquishing his leadership completely, as his actions only serve to thrust that leadership role right back into his wife's lap; and in the absence of leadership, she will certainly become the leader. As she continues to lead, he continues to become more angry and frustrated, prompting him to continue to withdraw, which continues to thrust her further into the leadership role! I think this would be a good time for us to all envision a cat chasing his own tail, working like crazy but getting nothing accomplished but exhaustion.

Now men, I certainly don't mean to imply that your wife will fall perfectly into your leadership role when you lead with love, as there is no perfection this side of Heaven. And I *do* realize that we women certainly have some control issues. In fact, whenever a man begins our marriage counseling session by trying to convince me of his wife's controlling ways, I always laugh and ask him to tell me something I don't already know!

But true leadership should *not* be based on the other person's *reactions*. That would be the definition of the verb "to follow," which Mr. Webster defines as "to come or go after."[4] The verb *lead* is defined as "to show the way, or direct the course of, by going before."[5]

Furthermore, when a man withdraws from his wife in anger or frustration, she will begin to feel unloved and alone. It is estimated that women typically use three times the number of words that men use daily. Men are far less communicative than women by nature, but as the tension rises, wives often "feel" that their husbands' lack of verbal communication means they are no longer interested in them or that they possibly no longer care. Ladies, we must get over this and not expect our men to suddenly communicate like a woman. We don't want them to become women, so let's not expect them to "chat" with us like a woman. Let's find a girlfriend for that!

WHEN A MAN LOVES A WOMAN

When a man leads his wife in love and sacrifice, will she be better able to *rest* in her husband's leadership, see him with the eyes of love, and respect in a new way? I believe so. Not only do I see this work regularly in my office, but as a woman who believes her husband would die for her, I would follow my husband anywhere and hang in with him time and again, even if I don't always agree with all of his choices. That's the natural response of a woman who feels *loved*.

Notice that in Ephesians 5:33, God tells husbands to love their wives as they love themselves. Could this be due to the sad occurrence in the Garden of Eden where Adam clearly loved and protected himself above Eve? Was God telling men to love and protect their wives even as they would love and protect themselves? Adam was a man—a sinner. He could not possibly exhibit the kind of self-sacrificial love that Christ Himself exhibited.

Okay, it's time for a trick question. Who do you think was the greatest leader throughout all of history? If you answered Jesus Himself, you scored correctly. In only three short years of ministry, He spread Christianity all over the globe. Our very calendars are set around Jesus' walk on earth—B.C. or Before Christ and A.D. meaning Anno Domini or in the year of the Lord.[6]

Next question. Who was the greatest servant throughout history? Once again, Jesus would be the answer. What is the most stunning way in which a person could serve me? By dying for me, of course. Here we see a second way in which husbands are instructed to love their wives. *"Husbands, love your wives, just as Christ loved the church and gave Himself up for her to make her holy..."* (Eph. 5:25-26).

So husbands are instructed to love their wives not only as they love "themselves" (see Eph. 5:33), but also as Christ loved His Church, His people. Essentially, husbands are told by God to love their wives by both *leading* their wives and *serving* their wives even unto death.

John 3:16 states, *"God so loved* [agaped] *the world that He gave His one and only Son."* There it is again, that sacrificial love. God so loved that He gave, He sacrificed. How does the knowledge of how God loves us stir in your heart? It makes me love Him back, praise Him, and thank and follow Him. When I feel that sacrificial love from my husband, I want to love him back, praise and respect him more, and adore and follow him. And what surfaces in us when we don't feel that love from our husband?

WHEN LOVE UNRAVELS

I think we can clearly see what happened to Adam and Eve. After Eve led the family and ate of the fruit, after Adam didn't take the reins of leadership to guide and protect his wife, and after they sinned and disobeyed God, their intimacy and vulnerability began to unravel. They began to distance themselves from one another, both physically and emotionally. It is such a tragedy when love no longer *protects, trusts, hopes, or perseveres.*

Adam and Eve's response was to cover themselves with *manmade* fig leaves so they could hide themselves from each other as well as from God. Why did they need to hide themselves? Before their sin, they could share everything that thrilled their hearts with their lover, every innocent desire, every carefree thought, without fearing any shame that their desires were tainted in self-centered motives or pride. Now that they had sinned, vulnerability was no longer safe. Pride began to place itself as a thin covering over the heart, making almost every future response to one another subject to a new filter that skews the most humble human at some juncture in the road.

OUR PRIDE TEARS AT THE SOUL

Oh, the heartbreaking words couples speak to one another, tearing at each other's souls all because their pride no longer allows them to just cry out to their lover for *love* or *respect*.

- "You're going to be home early tonight? Surrrrrrrrrrre you are."

- "Have we ever really had a special connection? I wonder."

- "I should have gotten to know you better before I ever agreed to marry you. No turning back the clock."

How difficult it is for couples to make simple forgiveness, simple. Without forgiveness, *no* relationship can possibly endure. Pride makes it a long, drawn-out affair, often causing more damage than the original offense. Pride creates in us the need to punish the one who has offended us. Pride keeps us from seeing the simple fact that we have married sinners, so expect them to sin. Now, let's get on with our lives. Pride continues to do exactly what it was intended to do by the enemy: distance us from one another and ultimately distance us from God. Pride is exactly what distanced satan, the most beautiful angel, from God Himself. Oswald Chambers stated in his classic book *My Utmost for His Highest*, "The majority of us have no ear for anything but ourselves, we cannot hear a thing God says."[7]

JUST THE FACTS, MA'AM

As I regularly listen to couples describe the details of problematic events in their lives, I continue to hear this veil of pride distort details, thereby creating their *own* perspectives rather than just reporting the facts. I remember an old TV program that ran reruns for years. It was called *Dragnet*, and the main character was a man named Jo Friday, a hair fact that my husband is a genius at remembering! One of the lines Jo repeated several times each show was, "Just the facts, Ma'am, just the facts."

Why did he have to repeat this line so often? Because people don't seem to be able to share a story without it going through the veil of self or pride. People would start blubbering to Sergeant Friday about how the "robber frightened their dog" or "disturbed their mother-in-law's nap, which makes her ever so ornery!" "Just the facts, Ma'am, just the facts," he would repeat again and again. How I wish we could rid ourselves of the *veil of pride* that makes it *impossible* to stick to only the facts. And as we rehearse our own stories to ourselves and to others, we continue to solidify them in our minds as truth rather than seeking God's *greater truths* in each story.

Today, when love wanes, the modern-day fig leaves include trips to the mall or the golf course, more time spent at the local bar where "everyone knows your name," or a myriad of committee meetings that keep us too busy to feel our emptiness, and of course there's always the TV or the computer to keep us from crying out to God or crying out to our spouse. But when a husband becomes the dragon slayer, the one who would lay his life down for his bride, I don't know a woman on this planet who wouldn't follow her husband's lead when she knows how readily he would sacrifice for her.

GLEN AND JULIE'S STORY

I must share a story about a couple I was seeing in my office. By the time they came to me, they had spent years on a marriage roller coaster that was nearing a marriage train wreck. Often marriages begin in bliss and then progressively begin to travel south, but this couple even began their life together in chaos and insecurity.

After several years of an on-again, off-again courtship, this couple finally decided to get married. Julie spent months planning the wedding, but then on their very wedding day, Glen backed out, leaving Julie with only a note of apology. Julie was of course devastated as well as humiliated, and yes, it was quite some time before Julie would even speak to Glen. But in time, she began to open up her heart to his numerous apologies, and then one day they just decided to go to the courthouse and get married.

How I wish their road could have smoothed out at this point. How I wish I could romantically declare that "love triumphs all!" But those early problems that had never really been dealt with began to resurface. Insecurities as to Glen's true level of commitment and desire for Julie began to plague this young bride. Did Glen back out of the wedding because of last-minute cold feet, or did he not really have that *till-death-do-us-part* love for Julie that every woman longs for? Did Glen go to the courthouse because of a moment of passion mixed with a spoonful of guilt, or did he suddenly realize he couldn't live without her? Sometimes while folding laundry, Julie would whimsically daydream about the wedding day she never had. Was their courthouse experience an omen of their *less-than-best* life together?

SILENCE CAN BE DEAFENING

As doubts and fears began to create a gap in their relationship, this couple began to feel that deafening distance between them. Glen sensed her distance but was unsure how to address it. He had already created such a shaky start that he felt it best to just keep things on the down low, not create any more problems, hoping that time would simply smooth out the rough patches. In other words, he withdrew rather than leading his family. But Glen's silence only caused Julie to confirm what she had suspected all along, that Glen was *never* madly in love with her as she had been with him.

As this sad cycle continued, so did the distancing. *Silence* and *distance* had replaced *intimacy* and *vulnerability*. Glen's pattern of withdrawal was 180 degrees opposite of the charge that God had given Glen—to lead! This cycle eventually led to marital separation as well as infidelity, once again confirming for both Julie and Glen that their love was never what each had hoped or longed for. They filed for a divorce, but in true Glen/Julie style, only 24 hours before the divorce was to be final, something caused them to halt the process and "try" one last time, if only for their 7-year-old son.

ONE LAST TRY

We began to explore the many ways Julie's lack of trust in Glen's love had caused her to question his choices, his motives, and his words. In time, Glen began to realize that when Julie angrily stated words like, "You always seem to have time for your tennis, but you never have time for me," she was actually crying out, "Do you love me Glen?" She was desperate for her prince to break his *silence* and declare his love for his bride. Glen sadly only saw her words as "complaining" or "nagging," which only caused him to further withdraw from Julie. That, in turn, made her feel less loved, which caused less communication, less joy, etc.

THE BREAKTHROUGH

Then one day the breakthrough came. We had been working very hard to reverse the backward direction this couple had been traveling. Rather than *silence* and *distance*, we were trying to create *intimacy* and *vulnerability* despite the way they felt, simply because that was God's blueprint for marriage. Making the right choice in life is often followed by the *feelings* that we can't seem to muster up on our own.

Glen was outside talking to his neighbor. Then without going in to kiss his wife good-bye, he simply got into his car and went to work. When Julie saw that he had left without a simple good-bye, those old feelings of rejection and confirmation that he didn't care about her feelings began to creep in. So Julie sent Glen a text message, "And good-bye to you too!" Old anger also began to fill Glen's thoughts, and in anger he did a u-turn to go back to tell Julie that as hard as he was trying, he couldn't seem to do anything right in her eyes. But as he pulled into the driveway, he suddenly did a u-turn in his mind, decided to *lead* in a new direction, went back into the house, put his arms around his wife, and kissed her, followed by a gentle, "I love you." Julie shared the story with me, tears streaming down her face. Then Glen's eyes teared ever so slightly as Julie shared, "I finally felt that he really loved me."

HE SLAYED THE DRAGON—HE PUT AWAY HIS PRIDE!

He had slain the dragon! He pushed away his pride, took charge of his home, protected his wife's sad heart, and won her love and trust. As we moved forward in our counseling, Julie felt a *yieldedness* and respect toward Glen, a love and respect for her husband. And isn't this exactly a man's greatest need? To be respected?

Respect to a man is like water in the desert. A man will search for respect in his wife's eyes, in her every response to him, her very tone of voice, and in her smile. I've often had a wife state in my office, "Well, I told him I was sorry." And he'll look astoundingly at me and say yes she did say *sorrrrry* in a screaming voice! A man becomes a magnet for whomever or whatever shows him respect. Why is a dog called a man's best friend? Because a man can just have rolled out of bed, unshaven, messed hair, and bad breath, but that dog treats his master as if he were the only person on the planet.

Why does God say wives *must* respect their husbands? Because God knows the heart of our men, and He knows what will most draw them into a love relationship with their wives, which is exactly the need of women—to be loved. As Glen began to show love to Julie, and as she began to show respect to Glen, this couple began their spiral *upward* rather than downward.

ONLY GOD'S WAY WORKS

When those needs of love and respect aren't met, Adam and Eve turned to carnal methods to soothe their pain, those old fig leaves we mentioned. But God clearly told them that their way wouldn't work. In Genesis 3:21 God instructs this couple that only God's way would cover their sin, their nakedness, their newfound loneliness. *"The Lord God made garments of skin for Adam and his wife and clothed them"* (Gen. 3:21).

Only with the shedding of blood can we be restored and feel whole and well again. Only the "shedding of blood," simply put, means that *only God's way* ever really works. The road to divorce is bloodied with men and women trying to fix their problems their way.

ADAM WAS SILENT

I recall a couple I worked with for some time in my office. Their marriage was one of the most painful I can remember. Their children were very confused and angry. Dad was one of the most hostile and defensive men I've yet to meet. He had stopped sleeping with his wife and was totally addicted to pornography of the vilest kind. When he came to counseling at all, he was generally rude to me or his wife. When he chose not to come, she and I would go over several circumstances from the prior two weeks trying to find ways she could show her husband respect—not his behaviors, but the man.

Then one week she came in sadly shaking her head and stated it was over; the marriage was finished. She shared with me that as long as she felt one shred of love from him, she was willing to keep trying to make the marriage work. But then one night, she had a tire blow out on the highway at about 10:30 at night. She was not quite 30 minutes from home, and felt quite fearful in the car alone, so she locked the car door and called her husband. Upon hearing her predicament, he cursed, using God's name, and told her he would have AAA come to find her, as he had only just gotten home himself and hadn't eaten yet. Her heart sank.

She stuffed her feelings and waited for the AAA truck, but she said she only wanted to scream out in pain in that car all alone. She used the very words that as long as she felt he was in some way her protector, it was enough love for her to continue trying to work on the marriage. But when even that was gone, she felt released from the marriage. He was distant. He was deafeningly *silent*. There's the heartbreak. There's the tragedy of Adam's silence.

QUESTIONS

1) Genesis 2:18 states that *"It is not good for the man to be alone."* What was some of the ways that you believe God was referring to?

2) Many women struggle with the term "helpmate" as they see it as a lesser role even though Galatians 3:28 states we are *"all one in Christ Jesus"*—male and female. Is this a struggle you have struggled with? Discuss.

3) Explain the difference of "agape love" and the way we describe "being in love" today. Refer to First John 3:16 if necessary.

4) How do you reconcile the term "servant leader"?

5) Have you struggled with making "simple forgiveness," simple?

Chapter 7

THE TRUTH ABOUT
SUFFERING AS AN
EXCUSE TO SIN

HAVE YOU EVER SUFFERED?

Have you ever suffered? If your answer is *no*, then just wait. Your turn will come. Mr. Webster defines to *suffer* as, "to undergo something painful or unpleasant, as injury, grief, loss, etc., to be afflicted."[1] Suffering is a *fact* of life. No one will get off this planet without some degree of suffering. Do some people endure far greater suffering than others? Of course. However, the real question for each one of us is what are *you* going to do with your suffering? Each one of us has a choice.

First, however, let's look at some of the ways we would practically define *suffering* in our modern-day society. "Something painful or unpleasant" could be a stubbed toe for a child, and look at how the child might react to such an event. Tears and wailing over what we might call a nonevent. But for most of us, prolonged physical illness or pain more appropriately defines suffering. Sexual or physical abuse can cause lifelong struggles and relationship suffering. Grief over the loss of a loved one due to death or divorce causes untold heartbreak and wounding. The sadness of the single who states he or she is suffering from loneliness, or the childless couple who aches for the laughter of children in their home, quietly cries "suffering." Financial loss can turn a person's world upside down, often creating suffering for an entire family.

Body, mind, and heart affliction due to verbally, physically, or sexually abusive relationships certainly places one in the category of deep suffering and is often accompanied by such confusion that its victims are often left in a paralyzed state. People often spend years quietly suffering from depression or anxiety because of the messages they heard in their youth that were contrary to the *truth*. From messages that communicated their worthlessness to messages that inflated them to a grandiose status, if they were not messages based on truth, the imprint these messages can make on the brain can lead to a host of relationship issues, which can possibly open the floodgates to suffering.

Whether our suffering originates from the seat of a physical condition or from a mental or emotional state, each one of us will suffer at some point in our lives. I'm certain each reader could recall their own shattered dreams, which have resulted in some form of suffering.

HOW DOES MAN REACT TO SUFFERING?

What is humankind's reaction to suffering? If we choose to listen to the world's *psychobabble*, we will use our suffering to provide ourselves with a myriad of "superficial psychological, shallow and not profound" explanations for our own poor choices and bad behavior. In other words, we will use our suffering as our *excuse* to sin. From a frustrating day at the office to the death of a child, from parents who divorced when we were young to our husbands not communicating with us as we need them to, it can all be used to allow us the easier road to do what we're naturally inclined to do anyway: to *sin*! And who among us doesn't want a good *excuse* to sin, doesn't want to blame someone or something else for our bad choices, our poor behavior? We saw it in the Garden of Eden as Eve blamed the serpent for her sin and Adam blamed Eve and God Himself for his choice to eat the forbidden fruit. I can't help but envision God chuckling as He penned out man's natural proclivity to blame others for their bad behavior as He states, *"A man's own folly ruins his life, yet his heart rages against the Lord"* (Prov. 19:3).

REACTIVE OR MALLEABLE

If we take that *short step*, that *psychobabble* answer from suffering to sin, rather than allowing that suffering to do something profound in our lives, we almost become a mirror reflection of the very word *psychobabble* with all its "shallow and not profound" simple reactions to life's struggles. We become *reactive* to the suffering and problems that life will inevitably bring rather than being *malleable* to what the Creator wants to do with us as a result of the suffering. We become a reflection of the *vast majority* who are always looking for excuses for their bad behavior, rather than that *small remnant* of individuals whose faith in God trusts even without seeing the end or reasons for the suffering.

How perfectly that describes the many men and women written about in God's Faith Hall of Fame from Hebrews 11. While some saw God do mighty feats, rescuing them from all kinds of horrors, such as the rescue of Daniel from the lion's mouth to the Red Sea opening to save the Israelites from certain death as Pharaoh's army was in pursuit to kill them, not all received that happy ending.

Some faced jeers and flogging, while still others were chained and put in prison. They were stoned; they were sawed in two; they were put to death by the sword. They

> *went about in sheepskins and goatskins, destitute, per-*
> *secuted and mistreated—**the world was not worthy of***
> ***them.*** *They wandered in deserts and mountains, and in*
> *caves and holes in the ground.*
>
> *These were all commended for their faith,* ***yet none of them***
> ***received what had been promised*** (Hebrews 11:36-39).

Not all of *us* will receive that happy ending with God whisking us out of our suffering. When we go through that period of suffering, or are perhaps still in that place of suffering, how do we react to it?

When I hear those words *the world was not worthy of them*, I can't help but see that *small remnant* who are walking with and trusting God in their suffering rather than the *vast majority* who will use their suffering to lash out, take revenge, try to punish or wound someone else, blame another or God Himself, etc. Which one are you?

THE BRAIN'S REACTION TO SUFFERING

The choice to sin as a *reaction* to suffering appeals to the most animalistic part of the human brain, the *amygdala*. It is this location in the brain that is responsible for fear, fight-flight responses, and most of our negative emotional states. It is the part of the brain that responds in a quick, protective manner, almost as an animal would respond automatically to protect itself, as animals are unable to employ reason. If you were to jump or make a sharp move toward a dog, he would instinctively prepare his body to defend himself. Growl at a dog, and he growls back. Spook a horse, and he rears up. Try to catch a bird or butterfly, and it flies away.

Such "instinctual behavior" and "defending territory" comes from the low part of the brain and is present in all lower animals, as well as humans. Automatically striking back, going directly to sin choices when you've been hurt or have suffered, uses that part of the brain that reacts instinctively in the same way animals react instinctively. So by *reacting to suffering with sin,* we are actually choosing to step down a few notches on the "food chain of intelligence." And while animals react to protect their bodies, humans usually react to protect what they hold most dear—their *pride.*

So too, with humans, our most shallow, animalistic response to hurt or suffering is to hurt back, to get even, to blame another, and ultimately to sin. However, the *truth* of the matter is that God gave man another option to instant reaction by giving only man the frontal lobe portion of the brain, the more complex *cortex.* The cortex is designed to logic, problem solve, discern, possibly try to do something wise or creative with the circumstances of life, and that would certainly include our suffering. God gave humans the logical cortex so we could use our suffering for some greater purpose, that we might grow to become more like Christ Himself.

AVOIDANCE MECHANISMS

Many people attempt to postpone or even avoid dealing with suffering altogether. This is nothing new. Alcohol abuse, drug abuse, rage aholic, eating disorders, shopaholic, workaholic, chocoholic (that would be me!), almost all have their roots in some kind of *avoidance* of suffering. While avoidance methods would appear less problematic, as such methods at least don't attack another person, they are still very unhealthy because avoidance once again isn't what God intended suffering to be used for. Avoidance methods usually backfire on the individual using these methods, causing increased problems for the individual as the suffering hasn't been able to be used for His greater purpose.

MARY TODD LINCOLN'S
LONG SUFFERING

Abraham Lincoln's wife, Mary Todd Lincoln, was overwhelmed with grief after the death of her son, Willie. For the next two years she *avoided* even entering the White House library, as it was one of her son's favorite rooms. She also engaged in shopaholic behavior that would rival anyone in my office today. She confided to a friend, Elizabeth Keckley, that she was in terrible debt to New York and Philadelphia merchants, unbeknownst to her husband Abraham Lincoln. "I owe altogether about 27 thousand dollars." This was in the 1860s! I can't imagine what that would look like on a credit card today. Then in 1862, Mrs. Lincoln began to hold séances at the White House and sought out spiritualists to communicate with her dead son, yet another sin choice to deal with her pain. Sadly, she was committed to an insane asylum in 1875 for several months and died in 1882 from a stroke.[2] Suffering will come to each one of us. What should we do with it?

THE APOSTLE PAUL

Avoiding having to deal with our suffering is nothing new among the Christian greats as well. Paul himself wanted a way out of his affliction, as we read in Scripture. Realistically, all of us would prefer to avoid the suffering side of life.

> *Three times I pleaded with the Lord to take it away from me. But He said to me, "My grace is sufficient for you, for My power is made perfect in weakness." Therefore I will boast all the more gladly about my weaknesses, so that Christ's power may rest on me. That is why, for Christ's sake, I delight in weaknesses, in insults, in hardships, in persecutions, in difficulties. For when I am weak, then I am strong (2 Corinthians 12:8-10).*

Paul was one of the rare few who *learned* to see his suffering as a *gift* from God rather than an excuse to sin. If we choose to view our inevitable suffering as God desires us to view it, we can grow into deeper, wiser, more compassionate people who walk with wellness and contentment, not perfection this side of heaven, but with a joy in our hearts regardless of our circumstances. If we choose to view our suffering as God intends us to view it, we will finish the race of life strong. We will thrill to hear those precious words from Matthew 25:21, "*Well done, good and faithful servant!*"

A SLOW AND DIFFICULT JOURNEY

This is not to imply that we can ever get to the well side of suffering overnight. It is a journey. It is a slow and difficult journey, but it is so worth the struggle. People who haven't undergone the journey of growing through their suffering, but have opted out in favor of the *psychobabble* shortcuts, will probably suffer more greatly, and with more cynicism, because with each suffering occurrence in their lives, they've never grasped the greater purpose, either for ourselves, for others, or for both.

> *And we know that in all things God works for the good of those who love Him, who have been called according to His purpose* (Romans 8:28).

> *You intended to harm me, but God intended it for good to accomplish what is now being done, the saving of many lives* (Genesis 50:20).

> *Surely it was for my benefit that I suffered such anguish. In Your love You kept me from the pit of destruction; You have put all my sins behind Your back* (Isaiah 38:17).

ROB'S STORY

Rob, a high school sophomore, sat in my office discussing the tragedy of his sexual abuse and the resulting fallout from that suffering. He experienced extreme anger at anyone who crossed his path, escapism from the lingering memories in the form of alcohol and drug abuse, and inability to concentrate on his school work, just to name a few.

One day I asked him what he was thinking of doing after high school graduation. He stated that for some reason, he had always wanted to become an EMT, an emergency medical technician. My heart leaped as I uttered the words, "So you've always had the desire to rescue other people in danger. Where do you think that desire came from?" As my eyes fixed on his, I watched this young man slowly lift his eyes from their usual gaze on the floor to meet me eyeball to eyeball. For the first time he seemed to grasp his greater purpose, his greater worth and dignity, coupled with a painful glimmer as to how it all originated. For the first time, he saw that his abuse had also birthed a desire to rescue others from danger, suffering, and heartbreak. For the first time, he realized he had a choice as to what he could do with his suffering.

> *"For I know the plans I have for you," declares the Lord, "plans to prosper you and not to harm you, plans to give you hope and a future"* (Jeremiah 29:11).

EVERY DAY IN MY OFFICE

I do not believe that a single day goes by in my office that I don't hear words such as the following:

- If she hadn't been so sarcastic, I never would have blown up.

- My parents always favored my sister, so why should I go by their rules?

- How can I show my husband respect when he's not respectable?

- My wife constantly makes a mountain out of a molehill concerning the kids, so I've just told them to come to me concerning decisions and not to even listen to their mother's crazy rules.

In each case, suffering, large or small, does not give the other party the right to sin. If we follow the logical progression of such choices, one would have to conclude that a problem would be never ending if we use our suffering or hurts as an excuse to sin. Why? Because if the second party decides to sin as a reaction choice, it will only invite the next reactionary sin to follow, prompting the next reactionary sin, and on and on we go blowing up relationships at a record pace!

In the case of sarcasm, why would we think that blowing up at the sarcastic person would make them *less* inclined to hurt another person with his or her biting words? Perhaps telling people how they have hurt you might prove more beneficial, as they might actually listen to you when you're not yelling at them! And just because they have spoken in a sinful and hurtful manner, why should you get on board and sin as well?

The second example concerning favoritism is one I hear often. If all kids who thought their parents favored one of their siblings used that hurt as their excuse to not obey their parents but simply "break the rules," most of our kids would end up doing jail time!

And if we waited until our husbands were completely respectable to show them respect, well then *no husband* would qualify for being shown respect, as we've all married sinners, and of course they are going to sin. Wives were never told by God to respect a husband's bad behaviors, but we were told to show the *man* respect.

And in our last example where we see a mom who "makes a mountain out of a molehill" concerning the kids, do you realize that this dad is actually teaching his children firsthand to sin against their mother, to sin against God Himself? Ephesians 6:1 states, *"Children, obey your parents in the Lord, for this is right."* And Exodus 20 states in commandment number five that we are to *"honor your father and your mother, so that you may live long in the land the Lord your God is giving you."* I actually told this dad that I would be afraid to drive in a car with him or stand next to him in a thunderstorm due to the seriousness of *his crime.*

Since God is unable to *bless* our sin, why on earth would we really think that sinning after we've been hurt or treated in a sinful manner could *ever* make anything better? I'm just too logical to believe such *a big, fat lie!*

NATALIE'S STORY

Natalie had separated from her husband. He had asked her to go to counseling to try to save the marriage. She refused to go to counseling with her husband, Randy, and stated that she wanted to go to a counselor alone. He contacted me to tell me that I should bill him for as many sessions as his wife needed. He told me that he believed his wife had been having an affair. He couldn't understand why else she would constantly be trying to pick a fight with him, trying to distance herself from him. She also had no sexual desire for her husband for quite some time. But Randy still loved his wife and wanted desperately to work through their problems, even if an affair was the source of their separation. He believed the relationship could be restored. He told me they were Christians, but his wife had not attended church for some time.

Natalie came into my office for her appointment. She was a stunning young woman with big brown eyes and thick auburn hair down to her shoulders. She spent most of her first session convincing me that she was only here to pacify her husband and to list all sorts of reasons why she was no longer with him. My concern with her reasoning was that her lists of complaints could apply to half of the married women in America! They didn't qualify as justifiable reasons to divorce her husband.

Then, after several sessions, she began to trust me, and the deeper truths of her tragedy began to unfold. At the age of 9, she was sexually assaulted by one of her older brother's friends. He filled this little girl's head with all the lies that keep sexual abusers in control of their victims. He told her no one would ever believe her, that her mom, dad, and brother would think that she was a troublemaker and crazy, that he would tell all her girlfriends terrible sexual things about her, that the police would only come to arrest her for her lies, etc. The list is too typically heartbreaking. And sadly, her parents were so absorbed in their own marriage arguments that they didn't pick up on any of the warning signs that might have stopped this cycle of abuse.

But Natalie had a sister in another state, and when she turned 14, she ran away from home and ended up on her sister's doorstep. She said she would never go back home again. While Natalie's parents were still in the dark about why she ran away and about the sexual abuse issues, they were so relieved she was safe that they agreed to let her live and go to school with her older sister.

While Natalie was safely away from her abuser, her big sister's apartment was no place for a young teenager with little to no supervision, and it wasn't before long that Natalie began hanging with a rough crowd. It's no surprise her first boyfriend was physically abusive. And so was her second. But in time, Natalie got her act together, graduated from high school, and then graduated from the local college with honors. She began to regain her self-worth by excelling at her job and being quickly promoted. She remembers meeting her husband at her first job after college graduation. "He was such a gentleman. I wasn't used to a man with such manners and kindness." They were married two years later.

THE EARLY BRAIN IMPRINT

How I wish this was the end to the story. But Natalie's former sufferings had made an imprint on her brain that began to shake her world.

Sadly, it is that *early brain imprint* that connects with *definition* of a given behavior. Let me explain further. I have several grandchildren. I can teach them what Grandma's computer looks like, what Grandma's glasses look like, what Grandma's candy dish looks like (I think they had that one straight out of the womb!), but how do I teach them, "this is what *love* looks like," "this is what *respect* looks like," "this is what *frustration* looks like"? The computer, glasses, and candy are all tangible items that a child can attach an image to that is physical and for the most part unchanging. But the intrinsic qualities such as love, respect, or frustration are invisible, without form or measurement, and are therefore completely subjective based on *learned* and *observed* behavior.

So how does a child learn what respect looks like? By observing how Mom and Dad react toward one another and toward them and the world. I am constantly getting parents in my office wanting their children to be more respectful and wanting me to suddenly teach them this wonderful characteristic at age 15. While I would never tell a parent it's too late, I do need to point out that they've probably learned what respect looks like by watching Mom and Dad's interaction with them and others over a period of many years. Something as simple as giving a child a warning about an unacceptable behavior, telling a child rather than yelling or screaming the words to a child that they are going to receive a spanking because of their continued disobedience, removing them to a private place for the spanking rather than spanking them in public or in front of family or friends, can actually *teach them* appropriate respect for one another. Times of discipline are wonderful *opportunities* to teach what these *intrinsic* qualities look like.

Frustration is another excellent example to teach an intrinsic characteristic. When Mom is on that aggravating telephone *"hold"* that we all dread, is she yelling about the "incompetence" of the company she is trying to contact? Is she throwing her pen or the phone book? When Dad is trying to fix the sprinkler system and finds he is totally over his head, does he start to swear and throw his tools or take it out on Mom when he goes into the house? We often wonder why our teen slams his or her bedroom door when he or she got a bad grade or had a fight with his or her best friend. While this is often a demonstration of rebellion and sin rearing its ugly head with a child who is testing his or her limits, we also know that it can be nothing more than learned behaviors from home.

The more important point here is that those early impressions or definitions of behaviors, both sinful and righteous, help each individual define and then emulate those behaviors. Meditate for just a moment on several other intrinsic qualities and how you might manifest those qualities.

HOW DO YOU MANIFEST EACH OF THESE?

- What does anger look like in your life?

- What do hurt feelings look like in your life?

- What does physical pain look like in your life?

- What does fear look like in your life?

- What does disagreement look like in your life?

- What does feeling insecure look like in your life?

- What does jealousy look like in your life?

- How do you demonstrate joy in your life?

- How do you react when you've failed at your goal?

- How do you react when you've been successful at your goal?

These are a handful of examples of how our behavior in various circumstances is most often based on the preconceived and observed behaviors of others during our learning years. This is nothing more than logical.

I had a young married man in my office some time ago, and I was explaining that *fights* with your spouse could actually be eliminated or at least a rare exception rather than a common occurrence. He responded by just bursting into laughter. After further discussion concerning his family of origin, *normal,* in his life as a child was one big yelling match, and now he was simply living out his *normal* using yelling and fighting to deal with every difficulty in his marriage. Sadly, he was also wondering why his marriage was about to blow up, when anyone on the outside could explain the problem to him in a New York minute!

BACK TO NATALIE'S STORY

So back to Natalie. How did she know what *love* looked like? What did love look like to her? Crazy as it might sound to some readers, it looked like abuse and volatility. That was what those early deeper feelings in her subliminal mind were whispering to her. That was *her* normal. Her first sexual experiences were bathed in abuse, deception, cruelty, and fear. Mom and Dad, who were supposed to love one another, were either in a "fight *du jour*" or they were not speaking to one another. This was followed up—confirmed, really, in her mind—with boyfriends she probably subliminally picked to mistreat her and verbally abuse her. Why? Because this was, after all, her *normal,* her definition of what *love looked* like.

But somewhere during those early years with her sister, she began to attend a church youth group and accepted Christ. It was the Holy Spirit who resided in her that was attracted to her current husband. Her husband was a gentle, loving, and clearly patient soul. Aren't these qualities that God Himself exhibits? What are the qualities God wants us to exhibit in our lives when we become followers of the Lord? Well, the *fruits of the Spirit,* of course: love, joy, peace, patience, kindness, goodness, faithfulness, gentleness, and self-control. The same Holy Spirit who lived in her also lived in her husband. Somewhere in that *new creation* called Natalie was birthed a *new normal* that was trying to emerge.

As Natalie would speak about her husband, she couldn't say enough fine things about him. But she did finally admit to having an affair, which she had hidden from her husband for some time. And, of course, what kind of man do you think she was drawn to? Her *old normal* was trying to call her back. She didn't understand why she couldn't stop thinking about her new love, why he thrilled her so.

This man was constantly threatening to expose her affair to her husband and her fellow employees, obviously causing her *fear* and *stress*. Several times when fights occurred, he was physically abusive, even to the extent that he threw her physically out of his apartment. He called her every crass name known. He saw to it that her money was often used for dinners out. How could it be that she was so drawn to this man? Her obsession for this abusive man and the guilt she felt for committing adultery, knowing that her husband would be devastated if he were to find out what she was doing, finally caused her to move out of the house that she and her husband had shared. She cried as she acknowledged that her husband "deserved better."

I must admit that I have *never* found a problem that enters my office that can't be found or answered in the Scriptures. They are the defining tools for every bit of my therapy. I use the same tools with every client because they work!

NATALIE'S ATTRACTION TO AN ABUSIVE MAN

We first looked at the logic of why Natalie was so attracted to this abusive man. Most people would begin with the statement, *She's nuts!* But the truth is that he represents love to her. He *is* her definition of love, her *normal* of what love looks like, based on that early imprint on her brain where love was abusive, deceitful, cruel, etc. There is an absolute logic to Natalie's *subliminal draw* to this abusive man based on Natalie's *subliminal definition* of love.

Remember that *subliminal* is defined as "below the threshold of consciousness or apprehension."[3] For example, anyone who has taught in a classroom can't help but recognize children who are starved for love. They often physically hang on the teacher, looking for constant touch or attention. They're not aware that their actions have surfaced out of a subliminal and desperate need for love that is perhaps not being met at home, but that need manifests itself nonetheless.

I've often observed the daughter of an alcoholic who never had a healthy emotional connection with her alcoholic dad go out and marry a very emotionally distant man. While she might state that she desperately wanted a man she could be emotionally connected to, that subliminal brain often directs people's actions and draws them to the very opposite of what they consciously want, but instead directs them to a partner with whom they are familiar. Her logical conscious mind would never have chosen that distant man. But the subliminal brain works beneath the logical and conscious-thinking mind.

While Natalie suffered terribly at the hands of sexual abuse in her youth, it was *that* very suffering that became intertwined with Natalie's subliminal definition of love. While Natalie never wanted the verbally abusive marriage that she saw her parents struggle in, once again that suffering aided in subliminally defining what a love relationship looks like. But does that give Natalie an excuse to sin against her husband and God? Does it give her a pass on continued destructive behaviors?

GOD DOESN'T HATE PSYCHOLOGY

While there is never an excuse to sin, I believe what we can clearly see is utter *confusion* in Natalie's life and thinking. She needs help from the Lord and His Word to sort out this chaos. God does not hate psychology, but wants humanity to use the study of the mind with all of its complications and bring it into alignment with God's *truth* that we might have order and healing in our lives, in Natalie's life.

Remember our earlier chapter outlining cognitive behavioral therapy (or CBT) and Philippians 4:8? CBT teaches that our *thoughts* birth our *feelings*, our feelings control our *physical sensations*, and our physical sensations control our *behavior*. In Natalie's case, her *thoughts* of what love looks like (abuse) control her feelings for this abusive man (she feels she's desperately in love with him), which controls her physical sensations (she's physically and sexually attracted to him), which she has let control her behavior, which is clearly the sin of adultery against her husband and God.

But this cycle is flawed right from the very beginning, as Natalie's *thoughts* of what *love* is are not *truth*! This will naturally flaw the remainder of the cycle—feelings, physical sensations, and behavior—which becomes the springboard for a shipwrecked life. Once again, it is that *lie* in the brain, the untrue belief that causes our disappointments, depression, and generally our messed up life.

WHAT ARE THE LEGS OF LOVE?

Our very first order of business is to help Natalie relearn the *truthful* definition for *love*, the one that has stood the test of time. When she can begin to meditate on the *truth,* when her thoughts concerning *love* begin to align with God's definition, it will begin the natural chain of events in the mind altering her *feelings* about love, her *physical sensations* about love, and her *behavior* regarding her reactions to what love looks like. *"This is how we know what love is: Jesus Christ laid down His life for us"* (1 John 3:16).

God is so gracious to simply hand us a straight-up definition for the meaning of love. When the brain is confused, as it is for most of us from time to time, we need only to turn to God's Word to get the scoop that has existed for all time, from ancient to modern times. Clearly, the *legs of love* are *sacrifice*. When others put *their* desires or even *their* needs aside for us, we know it's love. Isn't that what parenting is all about? Love and sacrifice? Isn't that what Christ did on the cross? Love and sacrifice?

People are constantly coming to me asking me to help them *feel* differently. Natalie stated that she wished she *felt* differently about her husband and about her lover. My job is to help people see that their feelings are a natural by-product of their thoughts; so the key to their changed feelings is to remove the confusion and constant questioning in their thinking and to bring their thinking into alignment with the Lord, into alignment with *truth*.

> *We demolish arguments and every pretension that sets itself up against the knowledge of God, and we take captive every thought to make it obedient to Christ* (2 Corinthians 10:5).

DEMOLISHING THE STRONGHOLDS THAT KEEP US IN BONDAGE

So how do we demolish those strongholds in Natalie's life that set themselves against the knowledge of God? (And I think we can all agree that Natalie's adultery is definitely "against the knowledge of God.") It is through the *mind*, through her *thoughts!* Choose to make those thoughts obedient to Christ and God's Word and the changed feelings and behavior will follow. Changing our thoughts and bringing them into biblical alignment will ultimately cause us to take a u-turn from the suffering, which *excuses* our sin, to suffering, which results in *glorifying* God!

And while many religious groups would simply tell Natalie to *stop it, stop the behavior*, digging into her past helps her to understand how she got to this confused place. I don't know that it's really possible to change behaviors until we understand what we're doing and why we're doing it! Without some kind of understanding, the body and mind are prone to return again and again to those old ways, to the *old man* that resides in each one of us. As Natalie began to realize that her *feelings* of love were coming from *thoughts* that were distorted, actually sick, she then realized that as we brought those thoughts of what love is supposed to look like into alignment with *truth,* it would naturally alter her feelings, physical sensations, and behavior. As she began to meditate on the *truth,* on what love truly is, she would recognize what is obvious to most of us, that love and abuse are opposites rather than connected. As she began to meditate on the *walking legs* of love, she began to recognize how deeply her husband truly loved her, how much he had *sacrificed his pride* to try to reach out and love and forgive his wife, and how many ways he had shown her love over their years together according to First Corinthians 13.

> *Love is patient, love is kind. It does not envy, it does not boast, it is not proud. It is not rude, it is not self-seeking, it is not easily angered, it keeps no record of wrongs. Love does not delight in evil but rejoices in truth. It always protects, always trusts, always hopes, always perseveres* (1 Corinthians 13:4-7).

AMAZING LOVE

What amazing love Natalie's husband had for her as he continued to *always* hope and *always* persevere even after the realization that she had been unfaithful to him. What amazing love Natalie began to comprehend as she realized how her husband had sacrificed for her. What amazing love Christ Himself showed for us as He sacrificed even His life for us on the cross.

When people allow feelings that are not based on truthful thoughts to be in the driver's seat, they will always allow their suffering to be their *excuse* to sin. When we give in to feelings to direct our behavior, we will allow those feelings to determine all sorts of thoughts, which we will use to rationalize every sin imaginable. We are responsible to *choose* the thoughts we place in our minds because those thoughts will direct our feelings accordingly. And when in doubt, God graciously gave us the greatest *how-to manual* ever known: the Bible.

MICHAEL'S STORY

Just last year I had a man named Michael in my office who had been having an affair. He stated that he really loved this woman and felt she was in his life to help him through a difficult period. Michael described this difficult period as one in which both his father and his brother had passed away. Michael felt such pressure as the newly assigned patriarch of the family. He was also experiencing a significant drop in his business at a time when he needed more income, as his father had not prepared very well financially for Michael's mom in the case of his death. Michael described himself and his family as "true Christians" and very active in leadership in their church.

I first tried to explore the *obvious,* which was, "Isn't that what God gave you a wife for, to be your helpmeet in difficult times?" At that point, he put up his hands for me to stop and declared, "There must have been a reason God brought this woman to me!" This seemingly intelligent man of high standing in his church had allowed his feelings of desire to take the driver's seat. He then began to methodically *choose thoughts,* which aligned to *his* own *desires,* that, when meditated on long enough, became his beliefs and then became his behaviors. Once Michael turned these desires into beliefs, he was able to use these nonbiblical beliefs to help him justify choices that most of us would find absurd—that most of us would roll over in laughter about.

For example, to think that *God* had presented this woman to him to *help* him through a difficult time is absolutely impossible because it is 180 degrees opposite of what the Bible teaches. And since the Bible's words are the very words out of God's mouth, if this man's chosen beliefs are contrary to the Bible, then they are contrary to God!

*When tempted, no one should say, "God is tempting me." For God cannot be tempted by evil, nor does He tempt anyone; but each one is tempted when, by **his own evil desire**, he is dragged away and enticed. Then, after desire has conceived, it gives birth to sin; and sin, when it is full-grown, gives birth to death* (James 1:13-15).

Based on this verse, God couldn't possibly have *presented* a woman to Michael who would tempt him toward adultery. Absurd! Instead, had his own *evil desire* for her caused him to be *enticed* and eventually give birth to the sin of adultery? Captain Obvious has just arrived in the building! Was this man heading in the direction of the *death* of his marriage, of the covenant relationship that God had established? Absolutely.

Had he been going through a period of suffering in his business as well as with his extended family members? Yes, he had. But by allowing his difficulties to help give him an excuse to do what he desired to do anyway, to sin, as that is man's nature, he had allowed himself a pass on sin that would eventually lead to *death*. By choosing to allow lies to enter his mind, by giving them fertile ground, watering, food, and meditation, Michael would actually be giving birth to the death of the relationship he had once had with his wife, he would eventually give birth to the death of the once-trusting relationship he had with his children, and he certainly would be giving birth to the death of the close relationship he had long ago shared with the Lord. If we choose to believe the lie that our suffering gives us an excuse to sin, we are only fooling ourselves and choosing a very sorry path.

> *As the rain and the snow come down from heaven, and do not return to it without watering the earth and making it bud and flourish, so that it yields seed from the sower and bread for the eater, so is My word that goes out from My mouth: It will not return to me empty, but will accomplish what I desire and achieve the purpose for which I sent it* (Isaiah 55:10-11).

Speaking the truth of God's Word is never wasted. It *always* accomplishes a purpose according to Isaiah 55:11. Sometimes that purpose is to draw us back to God. Sometimes the purpose is to reveal to us just how far we've run away from God.

My hope and heart's desire is that each time I present the *truth* of God's Word, each time I confront the lie, it will draw a person back to the truth that will result in the abundant life that we're all seeking. However, I am only the presenter. Each person determines his or her future based on what that individual chooses to do with that *truth*. Natalie chose to embrace God's *truth*, and over time and with help, her life has turned around. Last I heard, she and her husband were expecting their second child. Michael left my office and I have never seen him again.

QUESTIONS

1) Would you share with the group ways you feel you have had to go through suffering?

2) Discuss some of the ways people react to suffering.

3) Can you recall times you've prayed for your suffering to simply be removed from your life? Would you share some of these times?

4) What are some of the things you believe God wants to do with your suffering?

5) List and discuss some of the ways that we use our suffering as an excuse to sin.

Chapter 8

THE TRUTH ABOUT
GOD'S SOVEREIGNTY/
OWNERSHIP

A MOM AND DAD ASK WHY

Mom and Dad come into my office and begin to share their pain. They share with me that they are filled with rage yet, at the same time, their tears flood their bed, and they don't know how to stop the hurt. Their young preteen daughter, Jennie, was sexually molested in the park near their home. They describe her as such a sweetheart of a daughter who has loved being homeschooled because it has given her more time to spend with her mom and baby sister. Their neighborhood is upscale, and they've never seen anyone in the park who has even appeared to be the least bit questionable. The local police regularly patrol the area. This is a park that Jennie goes to all the time on her bike to meet her friends. The kids regularly play kickball or tennis, which are two of their daughter's favorites. Afterward, Jennie and her friends sit around on the picnic tables chatting and laughing.

One day, their daughter arrived before her friends. It was early afternoon on a beautiful, sunny day. A huge pile of sand had been placed in the park, which was apparently going to be spread around the playground area. Jennie heard laughter behind the pile of sand, and so she ran around to the other side, thinking that one or more of her friends were hiding from her. Sadly, she was met by a man, probably in his twenties, who grabbed her and sexually molested her. The act was probably stopped early when they heard the laughter and voices of several of her friends arriving at the park. Thank You, God!

Mom and Dad sat in tears. How could this happen to us? Why did God allow this to happen to our little girl? We love and serve the Lord. Is this some kind punishment on us, and, if so, why would it have to be taken out on our daughter? What did we do to warrant such treatment?

A GRANDMOTHER'S DILEMMA

A grandmother sits with me in tears sharing that her granddaughter is preparing to marry a young man who the grandmother is certain will only cause her granddaughter, Sarah, untold pain. She recognizes the warning signs of verbal abuse in this young man, mainly because her family's history is plagued with verbal as well as physical abuse. Grandmother states that Sarah is convinced her fiancée would never be harsh or cruel, as he has never unleashed such behavior on her. But grandmother is *certain* Sarah is not supposed to marry this young man because God couldn't have it in His will for her granddaughter to marry into a cycle of probable abuse. And while this young man occasionally goes to church with Sarah and her family, he has never stated that he has a relationship with the Lord Himself. But try as the grandmother might, Sarah will not listen. Now the relationship between Sarah and her grandmother has become so strained that they are hardly discussing anything about the wedding plans or the relationship.

Grandmother is praying and fasting each week for her granddaughter to "see the light," or for Sarah's fiancé to reveal his inner demons before it is too late and the marriage has taken place. She looks to me and asks the questions, "Is God even hearing me? This couldn't possibly be His will for her life. I'm old and tired and have served God faithfully. Why is God doing this to me? This granddaughter is more like a daughter to me, and it's breaking my heart."

A DAD'S SADDENED HEART

A dad enters my office extremely depressed. His wife passed away several years ago. He still struggles with her death because they were so in love. He has four adult children, two of whom live in the vicinity of his home. The other two children live out of state. He is pleased to state that his children all profess to be Christians, something he and his wife believed was more important than anything else when it came to their child rearing. He and his family lived a modest life, but his greatest joy was the closeness of his family and the camaraderie of his children. He has a whopping ten grandchildren and has the pictures and joyful pride to prove it.

However, in recent months he and one of his adult children have had a disagreement that has left this adult child choosing to withdraw himself and his children from his life unless his father concedes to agreeing with him in the disputed matter. He can't believe this is happening in his family, which was always so close and loving.

For the first time since the death of his wife, he is almost relieved she isn't alive to experience the pain of a family pulled apart by a foolish disagreement. "How will I handle maybe never seeing my son and grandchildren again? Should I agree with something I don't believe for the sake of appeasement? Is that what being a peacemaker is? Is that what the Lord would do? How could God allow this hurtful behavior when I've only ever loved and sacrificed for my family?"

IF GOD IS SOVEREIGN—WHY?

We've seen three scenarios. Each circumstance has left the client sad, lonely, and depressed. Each one is suffering from a broken heart and shattered dreams. Each one can't seem to get "unstuck" from their overwhelming feelings of pain. They can't get away from repetitive negative and sad thoughts. Each one is desperate for help from God, but none of them can move forward to begin the healing process mainly because they can't reconcile how a *sovereign* God could have possibly allowed such circumstances to befall them. "If God is truly sovereign, how could He have allowed this?" Why are these people "stuck"? What are the thoughts they continue to recycle like broken records that keep them where they are, and how can they get "unstuck"?

GOD'S SOVEREIGNTY AND OWNERSHIP

The reason these people are stuck is because of their wrong belief about God's sovereignty and how it is connected to God's ownership. So many people are quick to proclaim, "Of course God is sovereign," but somehow they don't want to connect sovereignty with ownership. The only way people will get *unstuck* and begin to heal is when they fill their thoughts with a more *realistic* and *truthful* understanding of who God is. Will we once again see that it is our unrealistic expectations, our belief in a lie, that causes us depression and anxiety? I believe we will. I see it every day.

Most Christians would state that God is *sovereign,* but what does that really mean? Mr. Webster defines *sovereign* as "above or superior to all others; chief; greatest; supreme."[1] What is interesting is that the word *sovereign* doesn't appear anywhere in the original King James Bible. This is because God's names actually proclaim His sovereignty. For example, the name *Adonai* or Lord, first used in Genesis 15:2, is actually defined as "sovereign, controller, lord, master, *owner.*"[2] A New Testament word for Lord seen in the Greek is the word *kurios,* which means, "Owner, master, owner."[3] The Lord *is* the very *essence* of *sovereignty.*

GOD'S SOVEREIGNTY IS NOT AN ATTRIBUTE ASSIGNED TO HIM BY MAN

This heading needs repeating, as it is at the crux of humanity's struggle, of humanity's lie concerning God's sovereignty and ownership. *God's sovereignty* is not an attribute assigned to Him by humankind. It is not a word we define in our dictionaries. It *is* who He is. Sovereign.

Logically, then, the sovereign one would be the one who is above all, who is the chief, controller, and *owner* of all things. Mr. Webster defines *ownership* as "the state of being an owner; legal right of possession or lawful title (of something)."[4]

The *lie* begins to creep into the brain out of the outpouring of human's greatest struggle, *pride!* While we give lip service to God being sovereign, *we* prefer envisioning sovereignty as an attribute of one who will administer fair and equitable justice, as we see justice based on our being good servants of the King. But the *truth* is that such thinking actually gives humanity control of their future to actually take ownership of their lives as they believe they can control God's choices based on their own choices to live a righteous or unrighteous life. Such a belief is contrary to the very word *sovereign* and results in humankind actually taking *ownership.*

Now, wait a minute, shouldn't we all aspire to live a righteous life? Of course, but if our belief is that we can have control over our future if we live a righteous life, it is a belief in a lie, a foolish and wrong belief not based on the truth of God's Word. It is contrary to an understanding of God's sovereignty and ownership, as they are inextricably linked.

And wasn't that what the Pharisees believed, that all of our behaviors determined God's favor on us? Isn't that the basis for all of our works-based religions? The harder we work, the better we look to the world on the outside, and the higher we move up on God's food chain of favor?

Such thinking actually creates a relationship whereby God is the servant and humankind is in control based upon our particular choices. If we're very bad, He should give us a very bad consequence. If we're very good, He should give us a very good consequence. Right there is where people begin their struggle. They believe if they have tried to be good, then of course a *good* and *sovereign* God wouldn't allow terrible harm to befall them. Once again, such a belief is contrary to the very word *sovereign*, as it puts humankind in control of their own lives.

SERVANTS DON'T DETERMINE OUTCOMES

But the truth is that servants don't determine outcomes; the Sovereign One determines outcomes. As we discussed in our earlier chapter on fairness, humanity is actually uncomfortable with a deeper understanding of sovereignty because it doesn't allow them to be in total control of their lives. If God is truly sovereign, then He owns us; we don't own Him. And that goes against humanity's pride. We like the word *sovereign* because it sounds lofty and righteous, but we hate the word *owner* because it makes us feel small and out of control.

When bad things really happen to *good* people, we panic because God's sovereignty isn't in accordance with *our* belief. Our panic only exists because, once again, we have believed a *lie*. The *truth* is that entire excellent books have been written about why bad things happen to good people. I hear it in my office every day. When we get to Heaven, if we still need help in our understanding, I believe God will supply that understanding. In the meantime, we must get out the lies and begin to focus on the *truth*. God is *sovereign,* and He *owns all* of creation. That makes us His servants, not the other way around. He is the Master.

I OWN NOTHING

The *truth* is that I own *nothing*. The truth is that our hearts struggle with this concept, and our feet have real trouble walking in it. We say we believe He owns everything, but sadly it is only when we're put to the test that we're really given the opportunity to come face to face with the reality of God's sovereignty, the death of *our ownership*. Only when our desires, our dreams, and our stuff is taken away are we able to see if we can give legs to the beliefs we profess.

God is sovereign and the provider of everything in our lives, but as our God generously provides for us, our prideful hearts begin to take possession and ownership with the clutching fingers of rationalization. I believe God will give each one of us opportunities to see what we truly believe when it comes to God's sovereignty and ownership. How will this *opportunity* present itself to us? In the form of a test, of course! Oh, shucks. I would prefer this opportunity be presented to me at the *spa*.

WHO OWNS MY BOAT?

On this week, I spent time with a couple experiencing terrible stress in their marriage. Their charges were so high that they needed a third income just to pay the interest on them. They were constantly bickering with one another about turning off lights and the expenses of new school shoes for the children. And then it came out in our conversation that they had an extremely expensive boat in their yard they were hardly able to use because the gas was so expensive.

When I asked with surprise why they hadn't tried to sell the boat, which would have paid off their charges in full, they sheepishly shared that they felt God had given them the boat, so they felt it was okay to keep it. At that point, I exclaimed, "How can you keep something that you don't even own? Perhaps God generously allowed you to buy it several years ago for the purpose of saving your marriage from disaster now. *Hmmmm.* Since God owns everything—your lives, your children, your home, your boat—I wonder what His priority would be: the covenant marriage relationship or the boat!"

THE TRUTH ABOUT JENNIE

Let's look at how we might attempt to better process young Jennie's sexual molestation. We begin by going back to Philippians 4:8, which is where we go for all depression issues. First, we *must* meditate on truth—*God's truth.* The truth is that this beautiful little girl doesn't belong to her parents. We have no ultimate control over her life. She belongs to God Himself. The truth is that if she were the only person on the planet, He would have died for her alone. The truth is that evil exists on this planet.

> *Put on the full armor of God so that you can take your stand against the devil's schemes. For our struggle is not against flesh and blood, but against the rulers, against the authorities, against the powers of this dark world and against the spiritual forces of evil in the heavenly realms* (Ephesians 6:11-12).

Until the day we step into Heaven, we will have to face the fact that evil is present. I don't like that, but I have no power to change it. The *truth* is that their daughter could have been killed, but God in His sovereignty spared her life. Let's meditate on that fact and begin to praise God for it. The *truth* is that this little girl is in a country and a home that will love and lift her up, see to it that she will get all the help that is possible as she works through this difficult tragedy. The truth is that this is not about punishment or what Mom and Dad did to deserve such a tragedy. God clearly states in Matthew 5:45, *"He causes His sun to rise on the evil and the good, and sends rain on the righteous and the unrighteous."*

God was brokenhearted when this was occurring as He was brokenhearted while His own Son was being tortured and crucified, but He didn't choose to stop His own Son's crucifixion. The truth is that we can't possibly understand all that goes on in this universe, but we do know that God is trustworthy.

> *But I am like an olive tree flourishing in the house of the God; I trust in God's unfailing love for ever and ever* (Psalm 52:8).

> *I will say of the Lord, "He is my refuge and my fortress, my God, in whom I trust"* (Psalm 91:2).

> *Surely God is my salvation; I will trust and not be afraid. The Lord, the Lord, is my strength and my song; He has become my salvation* (Isaiah 12:2).

The question is, Mom and Dad, do you realize that God owns your daughter and that He loves her more than you could possibly love her? Do you trust His sovereignty and ownership?

THE TRUTH GRANDMOTHER MUST MEDITATE ON

Let's look for the truths in our Grandmother and Sarah story. Once again, we must lean on the words found in Philippians 4:8. God instructs us to first meditate on what is *true*, then noble, righteous, pure, lovely, admirable, excellent, praiseworthy, and the God of peace will be with us. Once again, Grandmother must meditate on the truth that her granddaughter does not belong to her but to God. Grandmother asked why God is "doing this to her." But the truth is that this has nothing to do with Grandmother, as Sarah is her own person, not Mother or Grandmother's possession. She needs to meditate on the fact that God wants Sarah to experience great joy in her marriage and God generously gave her both a wonderful "instruction manual," the Bible, as well as the wisdom of godly family members and youth group friends who have all reminded Sarah that she is not to be "unequally yoked" or married to a nonbeliever. God clearly states:

> Do not be yoked together with unbelievers. For what do righteousness and wickedness have in common? Or what fellowship can light have with darkness? (2 Corinthians 6:14)

Then God even graciously gave Sarah a grandmother who regularly prays and fasts for this child. But the *truth* is that He also chose to give Sarah a free will to use as she chooses. Sarah has been warned about her choices. And the *truth* is that if Sarah knows her young man is not a fellow believer and she chooses to marry him regardless, she has fallen into sin. *"Anyone, then, who knows the good they ought to do and doesn't do it, sins"* (James 4:17).

The *truth* is also that while God is saddened with our choice to sin, and while He clearly forgives us when we ask His forgiveness, there are often consequences to our choices to sin that we must simply live with.

> But each one is tempted when, by his own evil desire, he is dragged away and enticed. Then, after desire has conceived, it gives birth to sin; and sin when it is full-grown, gives birth to death (James 1:14-15).

Does all this mean that God is not hearing Grandmother's prayers? Of course not!

> The Lord is a refuge for the oppressed, a stronghold in times of trouble. Those who know Your name will trust in You, for You, Lord have never forsaken those who seek You (Psalm 9:9-10).

But the truth is also that God is far more concerned with Sarah's holiness than He is with her happiness. And while I might not like that fact at first glance, could it be that as God moves Sarah toward holiness and relationship with Himself, only there will she find real joy, fulfillment, and happiness in her life? Could it be that if Sarah struggles in her marriage, she might draw closer to the Lord and experience a walk with Him that *is her* source of happiness? Could it be that since God loves her fiancé just as much as He loves Sarah (James 2:1 states, *"My brothers, as believers in our glorious Lord Jesus Christ, don't show favoritism."*), that God might have given Sarah the assignment of praying for her husband for the next 20 years and possibly seeing him eventually give his life to the Lord? While perhaps Sarah married her husband in disobedience to God, isn't the *truth* once again that,

> *And we know that in all things God works for the good of those who love Him, who have been called according to His purpose* (Romans 8:28).

The truth is that God wants to turn even our disobedience into good. And the truth is that if this young man does become verbally abusive, isn't it far more important to keep the doors of this relationship open rather than closed so that Grandmother can be a support and this young woman will not be physically alone? And here's what is lovely, admirable, praiseworthy, excellent, etc.: Sarah is a daughter of the King. He owns her, and He will never leave her. The question is, Grandmother, do you realize that God owns your granddaughter and loves her more than you could possibly love her? Do you trust His sovereignty and ownership?

GOD IS THERE FOR THE BROKENHEARTED

He heals the brokenhearted and binds up their wounds (Psalm 147:3).

Finally, let's look at our saddened dad who's not only still grieving the loss of his wife, but now he's possibly grieving the relationship loss of one of his children and his family. Once again, we must seek for the truths in this difficult scenario. We begin with Mr. Webster's definition of *peace*. He states it is the "freedom from disagreements of quarrels; harmony; concord."[5] Now, the problem we immediately have is that attaining peace in this world is actually contrary to the words of Jesus Himself, contrary to truth. Jesus states, *"I have told you these things, so that in Me you may have peace. In this world you will have trouble"* (John 16:33).

Well, right there we realize that peace will only be found in Jesus Himself. When Jesus says *"In this world you will have trouble,"* what does He mean? He means, *in this world you will have trouble!* Plan on it rather than carrying around *unrealistic expectations*, which will only lead to depression and anxiety.

The clear message we see from Christ is that peace will only "be found in Jesus Himself." And how do I have peace in Christ? When I hang with Him, lean on Him, draw my strength from Him rather than from the things of the world, do things His way rather than my way, etc. And that circles us right back around to Philippians 4:8, where we're told to meditate on that which is *true*, noble, right, pure, lovely, admirable, excellent, and praiseworthy. Put it into practice, and the God of peace will be with you. And the truth is that where in the Bible does God say that trouble will only occur with strangers, nonfamily members, and those we don't love? Sadly, it doesn't. Quite the contrary.

> *Jesus said to them, "Only in his hometown...and in his own house is a prophet without honor"* (Mark 6:4).

> *Do you think I came to bring peace on earth? No, I tell you, but division. From now on there will be five in one family divided against each other, three against two and*

two against three. They will be divided, father against son and son against father, mother against daughter and daughter against mother, mother-in-law against daughter-in-law and daughter-in-law against mother-in-law (Luke 12:51-53).

So our dad must flood his brain with truths to find peace. One thing we know to be true is that God loves the diversity of His people. He must, or why else would He have given each of us our own fingerprints, our own DNA, our own personalities—all of the things that make us unique. No two people are completely alike; no two brains and life circumstances are identical. Think about how many times we'll stand at our closets trying to "mix and match" various outfits, coordinating colors and styles, trying to make each outfit a bit unique to display our personalities.

With each individual, God amazingly "mixes and matches" every conceivable quality that makes us human, from our skin, hair, eyes, voices, intelligence levels, natural talents, interests, attention spans, charisma, birth locations—the list could go on and on. The uniqueness displayed with these varied qualities points to a Creator who is more multifaceted than the human mind can even begin to imagine.

The logical conclusion for humanity, however, is that each unique individual will see life through his or her individual lens. Will that different lens cause disagreements? Of course, plan on it. And when the disagreements come, lean on God's words.

If it is possible, as far as it depends on you, live at peace with everyone (Romans 12:18).

Let us therefore make every effort to do what leads to peace and to mutual edification (Romans 14:19).

Notice both verses tell us to *try* to rectify the disagreement. The truth is that we can't control others, and simply because we've birthed a child, that doesn't give us ownership or control over him or her once he or she had become an adult. We only have control over ourselves and can therefore only *try* to rectify disagreements.

But the greater truth that this dad needs to meditate on is that his son and family profess to belong to the Lord, which means that the Holy Spirit is alive and active in their lives. Disagreement should never trump truth; therefore, the Holy Spirit will be trying to convict them of the fifth commandment.

> *Honor your father and your mother, so that you may live long in the land the Lord your God is giving you* (Exodus 20:12).

If I could list the number of family disputes that enter my office, I would have to empty half my files. The truth is that we put such high expectations on family members, expecting them to feel a certain way, behave a certain way, and respond or speak in a certain way, and because of our *ownership* issues with family members, that *certain way* is usually *our certain way*. Instead, we need to be praying for the Holy Spirit to guide both ourselves as well as our family members.

Our dad must meditate on the truth that he was given the privilege of birthing and training these children as best he could for the purpose of releasing them to soar or struggle, or realistically to do a bit of both. Our dad must meditate on the truth that each person has been given a free will by God. Our dad must meditate on the greater *truth* that when we get to Heaven, we will finally achieve perfect peace. He must meditate on the truth that even if the disagreement is never healed on earth, he need not worry about tomorrow because life is only a blink in time, but eternity is something we can't even get our finite minds around.

Now listen, you who say, "Today or tomorrow we will go to this or that city, spend a year there, or carry on business and make money." Why, you do not even know what will happen tomorrow. What is your life? You are a mist that appears for a little while and then vanishes (James 4:13-14).

The truth is that for all eternity this dad will be able to spend time with his son and his grandchildren where there is perfect *peace*. The truth is that God is the only one who promised to never leave or forsake you, and He is waiting and wanting to comfort this dad if he'll just let Him. The question is, Dad, do you realize that God *owns* your son and loves him more than you could possibly love him? Do you realize that God *owns* and died for you as well and loves you more than you could ever imagine? Do you believe in and trust His sovereignty and ownership?

QUESTIONS

1) Define in your own words what "sovereignty" means to you.

2) Discuss the word "ownership" and compare and contrast it to the word "sovereignty."

3) How does our pride conflict with God's sovereignty/ownership?

4) How did the Pharisees' behaviors actually attempt to relegate God to being the "servant" rather than the "master?"

5) What do you own? Since you can't lose what you do not own, how can your "realistic expectations" help you to avoid disappointment?

Chapter 9

NEW TRUTHS ABOUT
THE BRAIN

THE SYMPATHETIC AND PARASYMPATHETIC NERVOUS SYSTEM AND FIRST THESSALONIANS 5:16

I absolutely love science. Mr. Webster defines *science* as "the state or fact of knowledge."[1] The word *fact* is defined as "that which is done; deed; fact." So as we study science, we are actually studying "the state or fact of knowledge, that which is done."[2] As we study the human body, we are studying collected facts about that human body. When we study the rain forest, we are studying information and facts collected from the rain forest. When we are studying air quality, we are studying the level of pathogens per cubic square foot of air space. As we study science, we are studying facts; we are studying truths. Therefore, the longer we study *truth,* the more it will inevitably lead us to God.

For years, humanity has been trying to ease God out of the science of human creation and the body. But at a recent seminar given by the Institute for Natural Resources, I was introduced to yet *another truth* linking the brain, the Bible, and the truth. The institute seminar taught about the sympathetic and parasympathetic nervous systems, but God gave us insights about these systems 2,000 years ago in First Thessalonians 5:16.

THE BODY CREATED FOR FIRST-CENTURY MAN

The body that we are all born with was actually designed to live in a world that no longer exists! We were originally created to be hunters and gatherers. Thousands of years ago, the average person walked approximately 20 miles per day, which is so unlike our high-caloric, low fat-burning, sedentary lifestyles of the twenty-first-century (INR). The body was designed with an automatic response system to manage acute stressors in our lives. A stressor those many years ago could have been the appearance of a tiger suddenly coming out from the bush. A stressor could also have been a step into quicksand, which demands immediate action, strength, clarity, etc., for the species to survive the crisis. Today, stressors, real or perceived, occur day in and day out, from stress at our jobs, to fear of not having enough money in the checking account, to the exhaustion of one too many "drop offs and pickups" at one too many sports events or school activities, to meals in the car while on the move, etc.

The human body is designed with an automatic nervous system (ANS) that regulates the involuntary functions of the body by connecting the central nervous system (the brain and spinal cord) to other organs of the body by way of an extensive network of nerve fibers. Involuntary body activities would include perspiration, heartbeat, blood pressure, breathing, pupil dilation or contraction, salivary gland stimulation, liver activity, etc. This automatic nervous system is composed of two opposing systems: the *sympathetic* and the *parasympathetic* nervous systems.

THE SYMPATHETIC SYSTEM
RESPONDS TO DANGER

The nerve fibers specifically created to react to dangerous or fearful situations are collectively called the sympathetic nervous system. The term was chosen to illustrate the *sympathizing relationship* between thinking (the brain) and feeling (visceral organs). The term was named by a Roman physician, Galen. This system is basically the body's automatic "stress response" to either *real* or *perceived dangers*. These dangers cause involuntary changes in the body as we experience anxiety or fear. If a tiger is stalking you in the jungle, you will experience a myriad of fear responses. If you think you *might* have failed one of your exams, you will very possibly experience many of the same physical responses.

These changes might include a rapid heartbeat when you're fearful. That alone has sent many a person to the emergency room for fear of a heart attack. It might include a muscle tightening when you're feeling stressed. That often leads to headaches. It might cause a quickening of your breathing if you're feeling dread, causing lightheadedness. In other words, the body *sympathizes* with the person's emotional state, comes alongside of the person, and *automatically* reacts to the person's stressful circumstances for the purpose of protecting the species as described in our chapter on *anxiety*.

EVERYONE CLOSE YOUR EYES

A good way to understand this automatic process is to close your eyes and envision yourself for just a moment driving on the turnpike at about 65 miles per hour. Now envision an 18-wheeler suddenly skipping over the road median and coming right toward you at the same speed! Your brain *knows* you're about to be hit. Would you gasp for breath? I suspect you would. This is part of the body's automatic system designed to protect itself. That one last big gulp of oxygen might just keep a person alive long enough until help comes if a car accident has occurred.

When the body's sympathetic nervous system is activated, the body creates a state of fear, anxiety, vigilance, activation, arousal, and mobilization. Now, look at how important it becomes to have these states activated if a tiger suddenly leaps out from behind a bush! The person who is *not* fearful, vigilant, or mobilized at such a moment will inevitably be Mr. Tiger's dinner. This sympathetic nervous system ignites behaviors of fright, fight, flight, and sex.

CHRONIC STRESS AGES THE BRAIN AND SHORTENS YOUR LIFE

The body actually manages such short-term and occasional stress very well. Our bodies were designed to deal with these occasions. However, the body was not designed to deal with prolonged stress day in and day out. Continued stress, what we would call *chronic stress*, discussed in the chapter on anxiety, creates an overload production of the body's stress hormone *cortisol*. When the sympathetic nervous system is continually activated, causing the body's automatic stress response, the overload production of cortisol can actually be damaging to both the brain and the body. *Chronic stress* due to *real* or *imagined* threats prematurely ages the brain and shortens life by leading to a number of serious systemic diseases (INR). The human body was *not* created to withstand chronic stress.

RETURNING THE BODY TO CALM— THE JOB OF THE PARASYMPATHETIC NERVOUS SYSTEM

The other set of nerve fibers originating from the automatic nervous system are for the purpose of returning the body to normal or calmer functioning. These are collectively called the *parasympathetic nervous system,* named because it "lies alongside sympathetic nervous system fibers"

(INR). This system automatically kicks in when the danger has passed and our fear has subsided. This would occur after we speared the tiger before he was able to attack us or after we were able to avert a collision with the oncoming truck. In today's world, it might occur after a person has lost his job but realizes that his unemployment will kick in, his resume is up to date, and he is excited to get out there to search for a new job.

When the parasympathetic system takes over, our heart rate would return to normal and our breathing would slow down. Our muscles would become less tense, making our bodies feel more relaxed. We would stop perspiring profusely. The blood pressure lowers. Glucose and insulin numbers drop. Blood is once again directed to digestion. In short, the body attempts to *restore* and *repair* itself. The body's behavior is geared to calm activities such as digestion, growth, sleep, and energy storage. These are all signs that the parasympathetic nervous system is now in control.

OPPOSITES MEANT TO COMPLEMENT

While these two parts of the automatic nervous system are opposite of one another, they are actually designed to complement one another, working together, to and fro, like a well-oiled machine. During times of stress, the sympathetic nervous system is in charge, preparing the body for a possible fight-or-flight situation and raising the body's awareness and ability to protect itself. Then, as the danger subsides, the parasympathetic nervous system automatically takes charge and returns the body to a normal and healthier state.

DR. ADLER'S BI-DIRECTIONAL BRAIN/IMMUNE STUDIES

In 1975, an experimental psychologist, Robert Adler coined the term *psychoneuroimmunology*, which is the field of study that connects the brain, emotions, stress, immune system, and disease.

Dr. Adler showed that learning could affect the immune functioning and that this relationship was bi-directional (i.e., the brain affects the immune system and the immune system affects the brain.).[3]

This knowledge is of monumental significance when we study depression, anxiety, mood disorders of any kind, immune disorders like chronic fatigue and fibromyalgia, and heart disease and cancer.

The immune system can be significantly influenced by the neurological activity of the brain, which can lead to various illnesses and diseases. For example, prolonged periods of hopeless or helpless thoughts concerning your life, or frustrated or angry thoughts concerning your marriage or work, can communicate illness, discouragement, or hopelessness to the brain. These hopeless, helpless, depressed thoughts will communicate hopeless, helpless messages to the brain, resulting in a depressed immune system that essentially slows down, quits trying, and "goes out to lunch"—what science would call a deficient immune system, which in turn can lead to increased illness.

Medical research continues to advance this mind and body connection. Dr. Lydia Blank, in her book on the connection between the type C personality and cancer, believes that if doctors find a cancerous skin melanoma in a totally illogical place—for example, under the armpit rather than on the forehead or arm—they are more than likely dealing with a C personality type. The C personality is a person who says *yes* when he or she really wants to say *no*. People with a type C personality have difficulty dealing with negative emotions, and their driving emotion is fear. An emotional conflict is present, lowering the immune system.

Fibromyalgia has often been linked with chronic fatigue syndrome, and while scientists are still baffled by this painful condition, a correlation has been made to childhood physical or sexual abuse in at least one of the four types of fibromyalgia. Abuse causes those hopeless feelings in the brain, which leads to depression, pain, and disability (IBP). Studies are continuing to show a correlation between depression and an impaired immune system (IBP).

NOT ONLY CAN THE BRAIN AFFECT THE IMMUNE SYSTEM, BUT THE IMMUNE SYSTEM CAN ALSO AFFECT THE BRAIN

Understanding this bi-directional relationship between the brain and the immune system teaches us that not only can the *brain affect the immune system,* but the *immune system can also affect the brain.* The immune system can have a significant influence on the brain. When the immune system has been compromised—for example, if you've gotten a nasty cold—the immune system can send signals to the brain that will affect a person's thoughts, mood, and behavior (INR). Within approximately two hours of the body's infection, the body demonstrates behaviors that imitate depression—lethargic behavior, reduced sexual activity, reduced exploration activity, increased anxiety, reduced food and water intake, and increased stress hormones, just to name a few. This is often called the body's "sickness response" and is the body's way of *defending itself from the infection.* This sickness response usually lasts eight to ten days or until the body is healed (INR).

THE BRAIN IS THE COMMAND CENTER

What we're continuing to see in so many scientific studies in this relatively new field of psychoneuroimmunology is that the mind and body are absolutely connected, and it is the *brain* that is the *command center* for the entire system. Science or the "state or fact of knowledge" is doing a marvelous job of proving to humankind what God enlightened us about thousands of years ago.

Now we're going to explore a verse God gave us in the first century that tried to give man a roadmap for a well life, mind, and body. Only in recent years has science been able to clearly observe and measure brain changes due to the advent of wave technology, which we will investigate. God gave us direction for how to think 2,000 years ago because He knew what would logically work best for the *mind and body connection* to give us "life and life abundant," which is His will for our lives. Two thousand years later science is catching up with God's wisdom. It is a verse that frankly used to annoy me because I felt it was so *unrealistic* and impossible to achieve: *"Be joyful always; pray continually; give thanks in all circumstances, for this is God's will for you in Christ Jesus"* (1 Thess. 5:16-18).

BE JOYFUL ALWAYS?

For many years I remember thinking it was impossible to *be joyful always*. How, God, can we be joyful for the death of a loved one or the loss of a job? But as I grew in my relationship with God, I did begin to *pray continually* simply because I was always in conversation with God. I began to find that the more I was in communication with God, the more happy or joyful I found I was becoming. How logical this is! I can remember many years ago when I first fell in love with my husband. I'm sure many of you can relate to this story. As I spent more and more time with him, I saw qualities in him that I admired, found endearing, and respected. I can still see him sitting on my parents' living room floor gently removing a thorn from our golden retriever's paw and thinking to myself, *Could there be a kinder or gentler man on earth?*

This is what happens when you spend time with the Lord. You continue to fall in love with a God whose attributes you can't help but be drawn to. He loves us sacrificially, is the Creator of this magnificent planet called Earth, is both righteous and merciful at the same time, is the essence of peace—the list could go on and on. The difference between these two loves—my husband and the Lord—is that eventually

I must see some of my husband's faults, as he must begin to see my faults. Why? Because we've each married a sinner so, of course, sin must eventually show itself. However, the more time I spend with God, the more I see His beauty and perfection. And the more I meditate on what is *"true, noble, right, pure, lovely, admirable, excellent and praiseworthy,"* as God instructed me to do in Philippians 4:8, the more I meditate on my husband's *attributes* rather than his *faults,* and the more I am logically happy and filled with joy and peace in my marriage.

GIVE THANKS IN ALL CIRCUMSTANCES?

So I came to admit that my joy has increased as I'm in a regular state of prayer. But then comes the tough part of that verse: *"Give thanks in all circumstances, for this is God's will for you in Christ Jesus"* (1 Thess. 5:18). Ouch! I'm a Jersey girl and frankly found it rather irritating when I would hear others praising God for horrible situations. When somebody lost a job, I often heard, "God must have something better planned for me," when my brain would be thinking, *Yeah, that probably means the unemployment line!* Perhaps I was just too cynical, practical, or something in between to grasp the "happy place."

As a therapist, I've had many a depressed client in my office who was praising God by holding onto that belief that "God must have something better," or "I just know God's going to heal me," only to see them end up losing their house to foreclosure or not end up healed. But God never promised something better will always come in the physical realm.

THE INSTITUTE FOR NATURAL RESOURCES

Then, at the Institute for Natural Resources seminar, I learned some wonderful new information concerning the brain. There were approximately 300 to 400 people in the convention center that day. Our lecturer explained that while we've sent men to the moon, we've been unable to study the brain in great depth, as science would like. While science is able to study the human body while a person is alive, cut into his body, do various procedures, close the person up, and have him walk away and tell about it, science is unable to cut through the human skull, poke around with various instruments, do some research, close you up, and have you a mentally well person. But since the advent of all the wave technology, like MRIs, CAT scans, PET scans, etc., science has been able to study brain activity in a way they've been unable to do for centuries.

THE MOST COMPLEX OBJECT ON EARTH

The *cortex* is the prefrontal portion part of the brain. It is the conscious, higher thinking part of the brain. It is located along the top portion of the brain. This is the place where comprehension of language, abstract thought, and usage of tools and processing of social behavior occurs. I think of it as the *input* location, as it is where all information first enters the brain, where we actually think about it, and where the original processing of circumstances occurs. It is also the location where stress begins. It is considered to be the most "complex object on earth exceeding in complexity any machine we have ever built." How interesting that it is *only found in humans* (INR).

Then we have the *limbic system* portion of the brain or the subconscious brain. This is the feeling portion of the brain. This is where information from the *cortex* is sent and where memories from that information are aroused through the *hippocampus* and the *amygdala*, which then assigns an emotion to the thought. The subconscious part of the brain refers to mental processes and reactions that occur without conscious awareness or perception, often thought to be *below* the threshold of conscious thinking. The major function of the *limbic system* is to control hormone production, memory, and mood in the species.

WOMEN HAVE A BIGGER HIPPOCAMPUS!

The *hippocampus* is a part of this system that forms memory and spatial memory. Once again, how interesting that this organ is *larger* in females than in males. Could this be a reason why women are always dredging up all those past mistakes and details when debating with their husbands? Most husbands I've dealt with in my office are convinced God gave their wives memories like elephants, including my own husband!

The amygdala is also part of this limbic system, and it is primarily responsible for fear, fight-or-flight responses, and anger. Essentially, it affects negative emotional states. What a shock that this organ is also larger in females than in males. Could this explain the considerably higher rates of depression in females? The *hypothalamus*, part of the *limbic system*, is the organ that most controls the endocrine system, which in turn regulates temperature, hunger, thirst, sexual arousal, and the sleep/wake cycle.

HOW THE CORTEX AND THE LIMBIC SYSTEM INTERACT

Let's look at how these two portions of the brain interact. It is through the *cortex* portion of the brain that I might process a message concerning a rainy day, but the *limbic system* assigns feelings to the message. For example, I might step outside and speak to myself, saying, "Wow, look at those storm clouds. How I love a pounding rain. I can still remember sitting with my grandma on the porch watching the wind and rain. It shines up all the leaves, and boy could our lawn use a good soaking. That sprinkler system just doesn't cover the entire lawn. Hmm—I better give myself an extra ten minutes to get home. Better to be safe than sorry!"

Or I might step outside and speak to myself, saying, "Oh, I bet we're going to get a storm. I'm so afraid to drive home in the rain. It was in the rain that I had my only car accident. I can still remember standing in that cold rain after the accident. Sure, the office is only two miles from the house, but that's where most accidents occur. I wonder if it's going to rain on the weekend as well. Probably—unlucky me."

THE EXACT SAME EVENT—NEGATIVE OR POSITIVE

This example shows the way a person chooses to process the exact same event in either a positive or a negative way. In this instance, the hippocampus assigned the memories, and the amygdala assigned the feelings. Notice that the circumstance—the truth, the fact—is that it is probably going to rain. That has been established. It is a fact that is *not* changing.

However, we've just watched a person make a choice about whether to send a positive or a negative message to the brain, which has nothing to do with the facts (rainy afternoon) but rather with the person's perception of the facts. In the first scenario, the person enjoys the rain and actually has fond memories of rainy days with Grandma. In the second scenario, the person has fearful memories of the rain and doesn't particularly enjoy rainy days. The important issue that contributes to a healthy brain and a correlating healthy body is the *message* that is going to the brain. Is it a message of fear, anger, hopelessness, and helplessness that will begin to signal the brain to prepare to protect itself?

IT'S NOT TOO LATE TO CHANGE HOW YOU'RE THINKING IN THE CORTEX

That fearful or angry message chosen by the individual will begin its processing journey in the cortex or the prefrontal lobe. Remember, this is the conscious-thinking part of the brain, where a person can still make a decision or *change* a way of thinking about a particular issue. While the brain might recall a car accident (truthful fact) on that rainy day, a person could speak a positive message of thankfulness and praise to God that He was so kind to protect him or her when he or she had a car accident on a rainy day. "Wow, seeing that rain coming reminds me how good You were, God, to spare my life when I could have been killed in my car accident on that rainy day. You must have more important assignments for me before I travel home to Your arms!" An *altered* message will also alter the message sent to the brain, which has now become *positive* and *calming* and yet *has not altered the truth one bit*—the truth that you did have a car accident on a rainy day.

100 BILLION STRONG

In this case, however, the person has chosen a fearful and generally negative way of viewing the circumstance, which is factual and will not change; it is going to rain. That negative interpretation of factual information is now picked up and delivered to the limbic portion (assigns feelings) of the brain by way of 100 billion electrically charged neurons or brain cells. These neurons are comprised of dendrites, which take in information, a cell body, and axons, which send out information. Each of the 100 billion neurons can house as many as 20,000 dendrites and axons, and these brain cells are constantly either conducting an electrical charge (excite) or not conducting the electrical charge (inhibit). The easiest way to understand this process is to think of these neurons as light switches; they are either on or off.

Neurotransmitters are the *chemical* messengers that actually pass between the neurons and are responsible for whether these neurons are conducting or inhibiting the electrical charge. If the message chosen in the *cortex* (thinking) is a fearful, angry, or negative message, fast-acting neurotransmitters signal messages to the body's limbic system (feelings) to activate the sympathetic nervous system to create a state of anxiety, fear, vigilance, and mobilization to protect the species. Corresponding body changes might include rapid heartbeat, rising blood pressure, quickening of your breathing, adrenalin and cortisol hormones beginning to pump into the body, etc.

However, that exact same circumstance concerning the rain storm, perceived by the *cortex* (thinking) as a positive rain storm, can be picked up by the neurotransmitters and can signal messages of wellness and calm to the body's limbic system (feelings), allowing the parasympathetic nervous system to be dominant. It is the parasympathetic system that promotes relaxation, lower heart and blood pressure rates, body repair, and restoration—generally, the opposite effects of the sympathetic system.

IT'S YOUR CHOICE

It is the message we choose in the brain's cortex region that either sets us up to trigger the stress response sympathetic nervous system or allows the calming parasympathetic nervous system to dominate. Is our message taking us to a place of fear or anxiety in the brain, thereby beginning the signals to the brain to prepare or protect itself, *or* are our messages going to create a relaxing effect on the brain, which contributes to the body's general well physical and emotional state?

The problem in today's society is that most of our stress is psychological stress caused by thinking about threats rather than experiencing actual threats themselves. *Actual* occasional stress due to an actual threat that arouses the sympathetic nervous system, averting a car accident, for example, is well managed by the body. But when we create psychological stress, or a continual thinking about threats, we enter the world of chronic stress, which not only damages our body and brain, but steals our lives, joy, and peace. And this is contrary to God's will for us. John 10:10 states:

> *The thief comes only to steal and kill and destroy; I have come that they may have life, and have it to the full.*

LET'S PULL IT ALL TOGETHER/FIRST GROUP OF SUBJECTS

Well, here's where we're going to pull together the truths linking the brain, the Bible, and the truth. At the seminar, our lecturer explained that because of the new wave technology—MRIs, CAT scans, PET scans, etc.—scientists are now able to see the firing of the neurons in the brain when the neurotransmitters are sending messages (conducting) and when they are not lighting up, indicating when they are not sending messages (inhibiting).

Studies began to study the brain's activities as various stimuli were introduced. Subjects were gathered and their brains monitored with the most recent technology to measure the firing off of neurons. Subjects were asked to list all the things that made them stressed, angry, anxious, etc. As these people made their lists, the scientists watched the neurons light up like fireflies.

This activity indicated that the information each person introduced into the cortex was being transmitted to the limbic system (feelings), which would in turn set the body up with a heightened stress level. The heightened stress level would be due to the introduction of information that was stressful, caused anger or anxiety, etc. The body was doing exactly what it was designed to do, which is to raise stress to protect itself. This in turn causes a rise in blood pressure, heart rate, increased levels of adrenalin, cortisol begins to pump through the body, etc.

The same subjects were then asked to list the many things that brought them joy, peace, pleasure, etc., and once again the scientists watched to see the cortex to neuron to limbic system, or the brain to emotion and body connection, be activated. But strangely, the neurons didn't light up, which meant that the cortex or thinking brain was *not* communicating well, relaxing thoughts to the limbic system (feelings) to bring the body to a restorative state.

SECOND GROUP OF SUBJECTS

Scientists then took a second set of subjects and had them begin by listing all of the things that brought them joy, happiness, pleasure, peace, etc. Once again they monitored the brain and observed a firing off of neurons, indicating that the cortex was transmitting the positive information to the limbic system (feelings) by way of the conducting neurons. This automatically causes the parasympathetic nervous system to bring the body to a well state of relaxation, healthy for both mind and body. The scientists then had this same group of subjects list all the things that made them stressed, angry, fearful, etc., which would have triggered the body's sympathetic nervous system to prepare for protection of the species (i.e., causing the blood pressure and heart rate to rise, creating anxiety and muscle tension, etc.). Interestingly, the neurons were *not* lighting up. For some reason, the brain was not communicating to the limbic system (feelings) to prepare for danger and protection of the species, which would automatically cause the heightened blood pressure, heart rate, etc.

CONCLUSION

The conclusion was that not only are the sympathetic and parasympathetic nervous systems unable to coexist, but the one that is dominant is the one that is ignited first. If we choose to view life's many difficult circumstances in a fearful, stressful, angry, or negative way, we will be signaling the body and mind to follow suit. If we first ignite the sympathetic nervous system, the fast-acting neurotransmitters that direct the anxious state remain in the body for at least 90 minutes while the slow-acting adrenal glucocorticoid hormones like cortisol last much longer. The well parasympathetic system cannot be activated until the sympathetic system is no longer activated. Conversely, if we have chosen to view those difficulties in life in some kind of a positive or calming way, the anxious sympathetic state is unable to be ignited because it is unable to coexist with the well parasympathetic state as long as that parasympathetic state is present.

Clearly, it is extremely beneficial to the body to find and practice a way to bring our thoughts to a positive place, thereby taking our body to a healthier, more relaxed state. Praise God in the circumstance, not necessarily for the circumstance (see 1 Thess. 5:16).

I believe we've made it clear how damaging the onslaught of negative and fearful thoughts are on the emotional state as well as on the brain, the body, and one's overall physical health. We've shown that a circumstance that might be negative for one person can actually be positive for another person. The issue is not the circumstance, but how a person chooses to perceive that circumstance. There is clearly a need for *"truthful, noble, righteous, pure, lovely, admirable, excellent and praiseworthy"* thoughts, if only to avoid living in a continual stress mode, which we've shown to be so damaging to life and body. How are we able to maintain those well thoughts in the chaotic and stressful environments that exist in today's society? Well, notice that First Thessalonians 5:16 instructs us to praise God *in* all circumstances, not *for* all circumstances.

What that means is that God instructed us 2,000 years ago to find reasons to praise God, to find the *truthful positives* even in difficult circumstances, thereby bringing us to a happier, more peaceful, and more physically healthy state!

He doesn't tell us to praise Him for the divorce we are currently going through, but we certainly can praise Him for the fact that throughout the divorce, He will never leave or forsake us. Perhaps no one else sees your husband's cruelty to you because he puts on such a good face in public. But we can praise God and rest in Him when we read First Corinthians 4:5:

> *Therefore judge nothing before the appointed time; wait till the Lord comes. He will bring to light what is hidden in darkness and will expose the motives of men's hearts. At that time each will receive his praise from God.*

> *Even the darkness will not be dark to You; the night will shine like the day, for the darkness is as light to You* (Psalm 139:12).

> *For the Lord searches every heart and understands every motive behind the thoughts* (1 Chronicles 28:9).

We can also praise Him for the beautiful children the marriage might have produced. We can praise Him that we live in a country that provides alimony and child support so our needs will be taken care of. We can't praise Him for the divorce, but we can praise Him for the possible extended family members, church family, or neighbors who have stood by us to give us some needed comfort or support.

We can't praise God for an alcoholic wife, but we can praise Him for the way He's drawn close to us in our time of pain. We can praise Him for teaching us the joys of intimacy with Him as we become true prayer warriors.

> *The Lord is close to the brokenhearted and saves those who are crushed in spirit* (Psalm 34:18).

Many are the woes of the wicked, but the Lord's unfailing
love surrounds the man who trusts in Him (Psalm 32:10).

We can't praise Him for losing a loved one to death, but we can certainly praise Him for all the time spent with that loved one and the gift of memory that God has given us that we might recall so many of those sweet times.

I found I was slipping into a low-grade depression after my mother's death. I considered her my best girlfriend. I began to apply First Thessalonians 5:16 to my own life. While I could not change this fact of death that each one of us will have to grapple with at some point—it is a truth that cannot be denied—I was able to begin praising God for all our sweet times, and for all the times we practically rolled on the floor with laughter, for all the times Mom was there for me and I was there for her.

I praise God that I was able to tell her when she was well that she must stay healthy because she was my *best girlfriend.* I praise God that she gave me words of wisdom and comfort, telling me that those little daughters of mine would one day become my *new* best friends after she was gone. And finally, I praise God that I will one day spend time again with my mom so I can tell her all the things that never were spoken. I now smile with every thought of her rather than sinking into sadness and depression.

BECAUSE HE LOVES US

Difficulty, stress, heartbreak, and anger will come to all of us, especially since we are living in such stressful times. However, the key to an abundant and well life is whether or not we choose to find something truthful in each circumstance that we can meditate on with praise on our lips as God has instructed us. What irony that science now touts wisdom about their medical advances concluding the importance of positive choices regarding our thoughts, which will lead in turn to a healthier brain and body. A good God gave us this instruction nearly 2,000 years ago. Why? Because He loves us.

QUESTIONS

1) List some of the stressors common to first-century humankind compared to the stressors of today.

2) How do prolonged periods of stress, hopeless or helpless messages to the brain, affect the body and the immune system?

3) First Thessalonians 5:16 states we should give thanks "in" all circumstances. It does not say give thanks "for" all circumstances. Discuss some examples whereby you can give thanks "in" a difficult circumstance rather than "for" the circumstance.

ENDNOTES

INTRODUCTION

1. *Socrates of Archives of Internal Medicine* (November 1992 Victoria Neufeldt (Ed.), Webster's New World Dictionary (1988), s.v. "psychobabble."), volume 152.

2. Neufeldt, Victoria. (Ed.) (1988). *Webster's New World Dictionary*, s.v. "psychobabble."

3. Ibid. s.v. "superficial."

4. Warren Wiersbe, *Bible Commentary Old Testament* (Nashville, TN: Thomas Nelson Publishers, 1991), 22.

5. Kenneth Barker (Ed.), *The NIV Study Bible* (Grand Rapids, MI: Zondervan, 1985), 23.

6. *Strong's Exhaustive Concordance* (McLean, VA: MacDonald Publishing Company, 1972), 18.

7. Warren Wiersbe, *Bible Commentary Old Testament,* 22.

CHAPTER 1

1. Melody Beattie, *Codependent No More,* 2nd ed. (Center City, MN: Hazelden, 1992), 36.

2. *Webster's New World Dictionary*, s.v. "relationship."

CHAPTER 2

1. Bob Murray, PhD and Alicia Fortinberry, MS, *Depression Facts and Stats: Depression Statistics and Depression Causes* (January 15, 2005).

2. David H. Barlow (Ed.), *Clinical Handbook of Psychological Disorders,* 2nd ed. (New York: The Guildford Press, 1993), 241

3. F.B. Minirth and P.D. Meier, *Happiness Is a Choice* (Grand Rapids, MI: Baker Book House, 1989), 107–8

4. *Webster's New World Dictionary*, s.v. "unreal."

5. David H. Barlow, *Clinical Handbook of Psychological Disorders,* 280–81.

CHAPTER 4

1. *Webster's New World Dictionary*, s.v. "fair."

2. Ibid. s.v. "unfair."

3. Ibid. s.v. "mercy."

4. Ibid. s.v. "grace."

CHAPTER 5

1. Ronald J. Comer, *Abnormal Psychology*, 2nd ed. (New York: W. H. Freeman and Company, 1995), 207.

2. *Webster's New World Dictionary*, s.v. "anxious."

3. Ibid. s.v. "panic."

4. Ibid. s.v. "hysterical."

5. Bruce Weber, "Natasha Richardson, Actress, Dies at 45," *The New York Times*, (March 19, 2009).

6. Jennifer Baker, *Institute of Professional Pyschology* (Springfield, Missouri: retrieved 2011).

7. Michael D. Spiegler and David C. Guevremont, *Contemporary Behavior Therapy*, 3rd ed. (Pacific Grove, CA: Brooks/Cole Publishing Company, 1998), 321–22.

8. *Webster's New World Dictionary*, s.v. "agoraphobia."

CHAPTER 6

1. Kenneth Barker, *The NIV Study Bible*, 9.

2. TLN: Total Living Network, (June 17, 2008). *Marriage: For Better or Worse.*

3. Spiros Zodhiates, ThD, *Hebrew-Greek Key Word Study Bible* (Chattanooga, TN: AMG Publishers, 1996), 1571.

4. *Webster's New World Dictionary*, s.v. "follow."

5. Ibid. s.v. "lead."

6. *Webster's New World Dictionary*, s.v. "Anno Domini."

7. Oswald Chambers, *My Utmost for His Highest* (Grand Rapids, MI: Discovery House Publishers, 1935), May 16.

CHAPTER 7

1. *Webster's New World Dictionary*, s.v. "suffering."

2. Mary Lincoln: Biography from Answers.com (retrieved 2009).

3. *Webster's New World Dictionary*, s.v. "subliminal."

CHAPTER 8

1. *Webster's New World Dictionary*, s.v. "sovereign."

2. *Strong's Exhaustive Concordance*, 8.

3. Spiros Zodhiates, *Hebrew-Greek Key Word Study Bible*, 1644.

4. *Webster's New World Dictionary*, s.v. "ownership."

5. Ibid. s.v. "peace."

CHAPTER 9

1. *Webster's New World Dictionary*, s.v. "science."

2. Ibid. s.v. "fact."

ABOUT THE AUTHOR

Kathy Martin, MSW and LCSW, is a Christian counselor and psychotherapist with a private practice in Palm Beach Gardens, Florida. She is both a counselor and an occasional speaker for the Heath Evans Foundation, which was established to AIDS victims of childhood sexual abuse, and she has been interviewed on TV and radio concerning sexual abuse issues. Kathy is also on the counselor's referral list for the well-known Christian organization Focus on the Family. She is a former adjunct professor at Palm Beach Atlantic College, has worked at the Henderson Mental Health Clinic and the Children's Home Society, and spent several years as a volunteer counselor at First Care Pregnancy Center.

While Kathy did her graduate work at Florida State University, she also took Bible courses at Palm Beach Atlantic College and Moody Evening Bible School. She has taught and attended many Bible studies and now combines scriptural principles with cognitive tools to tackle life's difficult problems for the world's "walking wounded."

Kathy and her husband of 40 years, Ron, moved to Florida from New Jersey and Massachusetts. The couple has three married daughters and eight grandchildren. They have been residents of Palm Beach Gardens for 30 years. Kathy can be contacted at her e-mail address, ksmartinbook@yahoo.com.

In the right hands, This Book will Change Lives!

Most of the people who need this message will not be looking for this book. To change their lives, you need to put a copy of this book in their hands.

> *But others (seeds) fell into good ground, and brought forth fruit, some a hundred-fold, some sixty-fold, some thirty-fold* (Matthew 13:8).

Our ministry is constantly seeking methods to find the good ground, the people who need this anointed message to change their lives. Will you help us reach these people?

> *Remember this—a farmer who plants only a few seeds will get a small crop. But the one who plants generously will get a generous crop* (2 Corinthians 9:6).

EXTEND THIS MINISTRY BY SOWING
3 BOOKS, 5 BOOKS, 10 BOOKS, OR MORE TODAY,
AND BECOME A LIFE CHANGER!

Thank you,

Don Nori Sr., Founder
Destiny Image
Since 1982

DESTINY IMAGE PUBLISHERS, INC.

"Promoting Inspired Lives."

VISIT OUR NEW SITE HOME AT
WWW.DESTINYIMAGE.COM

FREE SUBSCRIPTION TO DI NEWSLETTER

Receive free unpublished articles by top DI authors, exclusive
discounts, and free downloads from our best and newest books.

Visit www.destinyimage.com to subscribe.

Write to:	Destiny Image
	P.O. Box 310
	Shippensburg, PA 17257-0310
Call:	1-800-722-6774
Email:	orders@destinyimage.com

For a complete list of our titles or to place an order
online, visit www.destinyimage.com.